PERFECT POTS FOR SMALL SPACES

PERFECT POTS FOR SMALL SPACES

20 creative container gardening projects

GEORGE CARTER

photography by Marianne Majerus

This edition published in 2019 by CICO Books
An imprint of Ryland Peters & Small Ltd
20–21 Jockey's Fields, London WC1R 4BW
341 E 116th St, New York, NY 10029
www.rylandpeters.com

First published in 1997 by Ryland Peters & Small, Inc. as *Gardening with Containers* and reissued with amendments in 2004 as *Containers*.

10 9 8 7 6 5 4 3 2 1

A CIP catalog for this book is available from the Library of Congress and the British Library.

ISBN 978 1 78249 636 6

Printed in China.

Illustrations *Michael Hill*
Designer *Sarah Walden*
Production *David Hearn*
Art director *Sally Powell*
Publishing manager *Penny Craig*
Publisher *Cindy Richards*

contents

introduction

Growing plants in containers, like all gardening, is a compromise between nature and artifice. It enables you to simulate all kinds of growing conditions, place plants wherever they are wanted, grow combinations that would be impossible together in the open ground, and overwinter tender plants under cover. Container growing also makes it possible to rearrange the outside look of your home in much the same way as you might rearrange the interior—to make a radical change to its seasonal appearance, for example, or to transform a terrace for a new purpose.

The projects in this book do not just look at conventional containers. There are ideas for portable plant screens—the equivalent of hedges in container gardening—for architectural containers, and for the plant pot as gate pier. The projects not only show how to grow in containers but also suggest how to place plants in an overall garden or backyard design.

There are innovative schemes for transforming an ordinary window box, terra-cotta pot, or wooden tub—simple changes that make containers relate to their setting. This is gardening as exterior decoration as well as horticulture.

George Carter

terra cotta

There are many variations in the color of terra cotta—from the harsh red of new machine-made pots to the softer texture prevalent in hand-thrown pots. The 18th-century English landscape gardener Humphry Repton used pale stone paints and lime washes to disguise red brick, which he thought too warm a color against the various greens of the landscape. Paints can be used for various effects, including making a container appear more or less conspicuous. The combination of white, gray, and blue shown opposite recalls the delft flower pots much used in 17th- and 18th-century gardens to set in rows on walls or terraces.

top A hand-thrown urn painted dark green has patinated to a mottled bronze color. Planted with hydrangeas, the urn looks best displayed above ground level on a painted wooden plinth.

above Clipped box (*Buxus sempervirens*) is a valuable container plant since its effect stays the same through the year. An underplanting of pink and purple petunias gives the box a colorful border in the summer flowering months. The petunias will need liquid-feeding to keep them going during the growing season in the face of competition from the box.

right The tall and distinctive shape of these pots is emphasized by their white-painted exteriors, which read better from a distance than darker terra cotta.

above A wide urn-shaped pot suits the spreading habit of the variegated hosta (*Hosta sieboldiana* 'Frances Williams'), whose bold architectural foliage continues throughout the growing season, making it an asset even after the flowers have died off.

above right This large terra-cotta pot has been planted for early spring with dark blue and white hyacinths.

right A painted stepladder makes a stage for a late spring/early summer display of felicia, drumstick primulas (*Primula denticulata*), marguerites (*Argyranthemum frutescens*), and double daises (*Bellis perennis*).

far right, above Machine-made terra-cotta pots have been painted in white, gray, and blue latex. Choose plants that sit comfortably with the color of your painted pot.

far right, below Dwarf tulips make a good spring plant for this simple terra-cotta pot. The double early *Tulipa* 'Schoonoord' shown here will provide long-lasting flowers in April.

terra cotta with a patina

Many modern terra-cotta pots, especially machine-made ones, have a raw new look that can detract from the effect of an attractive planting plan. They can also look out of place next to old containers that have been softened with age. One answer is to tone down new pots using an antiquing kit that simulates a patina. This project shows how to age a terra-cotta trough artificially using this method, and how to display the trough effectively side by side with pots that have a natural patina.

MATERIALS & EQUIPMENT

1 new terra-cotta trough 9 x 9 x 24 in (230 x 230 x 600 mm)
2 terra-cotta pots with a natural patina 10 in (250 mm) in diameter
terra-cotta antiquing kit
small paintbrush
scrub brush
bucket
20 quarts (20 liters) potting soil
pot shards
3 creeping soft grass (*Holcus mollis* 'Albovariegatus')
in 6 in (150 mm) diameter pots
2 balls of boxwood (*Buxus sempervirens*) in 1 or 2 gallon (5 or 10 liter) pots

1 Prepare the antiquing kit as directed on the package.

2 Apply the "patina" with a small paintbrush. Take care to paint right into the curves and indents on the relief detail.

3 Once the medium is dry, you can scrub it off using a stiff brush dipped into a bucket of cold water. The object is to leave a white deposit in the relief detail and around all of the edges, but to remove almost all of the paint from the flat surfaces, except for the odd blemish. You need not worry about scrubbing off all the medium because it sinks into the pores of the terra cotta, ensuring that a subtle color change always remains.

4 Cover the bottom of the trough with pot shards. Cover this layer with enough moistened potting soil to raise the top of the grass pots to 1 in (25 mm) below the top edge of the container.

5 Remove the grasses from their pots and place them on the soil layer, then fill the remaining space with soil and pack it down gently. Soak the compost and check frequently to make sure it has not dried out. After eight weeks or so, apply a weak liquid fertilizer. Continue to feed each month in spring, summer, and fall.

6 Line the bases of the 10 in (250 mm) pots with pot shards. Plant the boxwood, filling the pots with soil and packing it firmly.

7 Display these pots on either side of the trough. The naturally aged appearance of the terra-cotta pots develops only after several years of use out of doors. However, the artificially patinated trough, which has been instantly aged, sits well between them

alternative effect

An antiqued bronze effect, although more complicated than the patinated trough, is still easy to achieve.

Create a glaze by mixing one part water to one part deep blue-green latex paint. Wipe it over the outside of the trough with a rag.

Create two more glazes as before with pale blue and pale green latex paint and apply them in random strokes, with a small brush. Dip the brush in water and drag it around the rim, letting the water run down the trough in streaks. Allow to dry. Blend the glazes with fine-grade steel wool.

Finally, make a glaze with white latex paint and apply a thin coat to the surface of the trough; while the paint is still wet, wipe it off with a damp cloth, leaving small deposits in the molding and just enough to soften the colors.

painted pots

Paint effects can be used to disguise the sometimes rather harsh-looking red appearance of modern terra-cotta pots that have been made by machine. Use the colors chosen here or pick your own combinations to match the architectural background of your garden. To create the greatest impact, paint the pots in simple striking designs and select plants to harmonize with the overall color scheme.

MATERIALS & EQUIPMENT

machine-made terra-cotta pots: 2 with 9 in (230 mm) diameters;
2 with 7 in (170 mm) diameters; 2 with 6 in (150 mm) diameters

1 quart (1 liter) each yellow matt emulsion and palm-green matt emulsion

masking tape 1 in (25mm) wide

paintbrush and watercolor brush

pot shards

30 quarts (30 liters) general-purpose compost

10 lilies (*Lilium* 'Reinesse')

10 creamy *Osteospermum* 'Buttermilk'

6 lime-and-cream petunias

1 Begin by painting one of each size of pot in green; coat the outside and the top 1½ in (40 mm) on the inside. Repeat for the remaining pots using the yellow paint; you may find that it takes two coats of yellow to hide the terra-cotta coloring underneath. Wait for the paint to dry before applying the pattern.

2 Use the largest pots for the zigzag design. Divide the circumference at the base into five equal parts and mark with a pencil. Then divide the top into five, placing these marks exactly in between the ones already made around the base.

3 Apply the masking tape in strips, joining the top and bottom marks so that a zigzag pattern is formed on the outside of the pots.

4 On the outside, paint the green-based pot yellow, overlapping the edges of the masking tape, and paint the yellow-based pot green. When the paint is completely dry, peel off the tape to reveal a neat zigzag pattern.

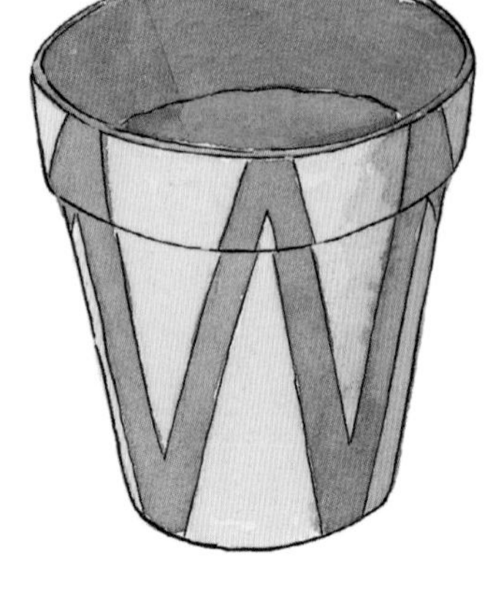

5 Select another yellow pot and a green pot and decorate with 1 in (25 mm) spots in the contrasting color using a watercolor brush; draw freehand or make a template by cutting a circle out of a 4 in (100 mm) square of card and painting over it.

Finish the pots by painting the top band in the same color as the spots.

6 In this arrangement the other two pots have been left plain, but you can devise any pattern of your choice, remembering that simple bold designs work best. Here are some alternatives.

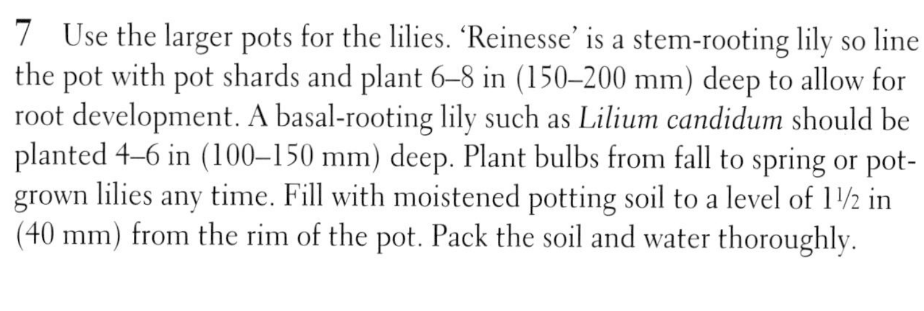

7 Use the larger pots for the lilies. 'Reinesse' is a stem-rooting lily so line the pot with pot shards and plant 6–8 in (150–200 mm) deep to allow for root development. A basal-rooting lily such as *Lilium candidum* should be planted 4–6 in (100–150 mm) deep. Plant bulbs from fall to spring or pot-grown lilies any time. Fill with moistened potting soil to a level of 1½ in (40 mm) from the rim of the pot. Pack the soil and water thoroughly.

8 Line two more pots with pot shards and fill with potting soil so the osteospermums (five per pot) are about 1½ in (40 mm) below the rim of the pot. Pack the soil and water thoroughly.

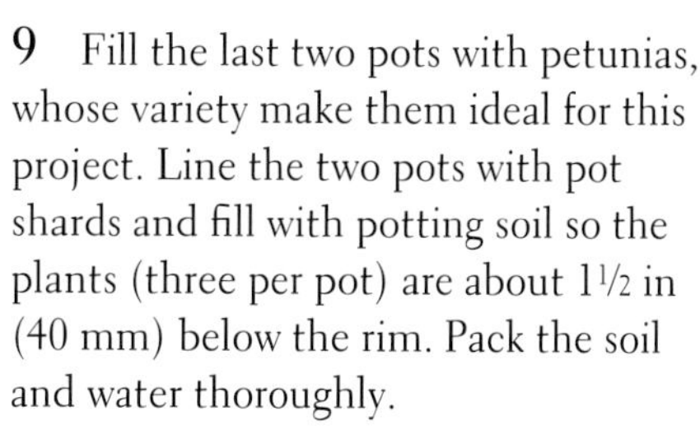

9 Fill the last two pots with petunias, whose variety make them ideal for this project. Line the two pots with pot shards and fill with potting soil so the plants (three per pot) are about 1½ in (40 mm) below the rim. Pack the soil and water thoroughly.

grouping terra-cotta pots

To achieve a satisfactory grouping of plants in pots requires planning. Limit your choice to a single material to give harmony, but select a variety of sizes and shapes. Mix textures and scales with seasonally changing flowers. Pick a plain background for a visually complex group, or a more decorative one for a simple bold display. The focus in this project is on the wide variety of pots and plants available for creating a group display. Follow the steps exactly or adapt the plants and pot sizes to suit the style and architecture of your garden.

MATERIALS & EQUIPMENT

large pot 14 in (350 mm) high with 16 in (400 mm) diameter
medium pot 10 in (250 mm) high with 10 in (250 mm) diameter
basket weave pot 14 in (350 mm) high with 14 in (350 mm) diameter
square container 14 in (350 mm)
small pot 7 in (170 mm) high with 10 in (250 mm) diameter
very large pot 16 in (400 mm) high with 18 in (450 mm) diameter
small cylinder with handles 12 in (300 mm) high with 14 in (350 mm) diameter
small shallow pan 15 in (130 mm) high with 12 in (300 mm) diameter
large shallow pan 7 in (170 mm) high with 18 in (450 mm) diameter
manure, pot shards, and potting soil (see pages 20–21 for different types)
bamboo canes • garden ties • spiral-shaped wire frame (optional)

spring planting

1 Fill the large pot with a young *Polygala myrtifolia*, ideal for training. Line the container with pot shards and plant the root ball in potting soil. Support the leading stem on a cane and cut off the tip when it reaches about 22 in (550 mm) high. Remove any lower shoots back to the stem and trim the ends of the horizontals to encourage bushiness. Once the required shape is achieved, clip annually to maintain shape. Protect inside in winter.

2 Plant the medium pot with hart's tongue fern (*Phyllitis scolopendrium*). Use a peat-based potting medium mixed with sand after lining the container with pot shards. Water regularly and protect inside in winter.

3 Plant a box (*Buxus sempervirens*) in the basket-weave pot; the simple shape of this plant sets off the patterned pot to its best advantage. Place a small pot-grown specimen in potting soil, over a layer of pot shards; keep well watered and feed with a slow-release granular fertilizer and spray-on foliar feed, to encourage growth. As it grows, pinch off the end shoots for a dense bushy effect and trim to create a ball shape.

4 In this arrangement two hostas have been chosen for their luscious foliage. Use the square container for a *Hosta sieboldiana* var. *elegans* and the small pot for a *Hosta fortunei* var. *aureomarginata*. Plant over pot shards in rich soil; use one part manure to three parts potting soil. Water regularly and apply liquid manure to plants in flower.

5 The evergreen small-leaved holly (*Ilex crenata*) is planted in the very large pot and makes an ideal subject for topiary. Choose a plant with a straight stem and plant in potting soil over a layer of pot shards. Tie the stem to a cane about 36 in (900 mm) long and grow the plant into the shape of a pyramid. Once you have a dense pyramid of holly, trim to form a spiral. Alternatively, train the young stem onto a spiral wire frame, attaching it with garden ties. Pinch out the ends and trim to desired shape as before.

6 Next plant the small cylinder with a *Hydrangea macrophylla* 'Blue Wave.' Line your pot with pot shards and plant in potting soil. Water well during the growing season and prune in fall. The color of this plant varies according to soil type; more alkaline soils produce the pinker flowers, seen left.

summer planting

7 *Ageratum houstonianum* have been chosen for the small shallow pan. Buy five plants in 3 in (80 mm) pots; the colors range from blues and purples to pinks and whites. In late May line the pan with pot shards and arrange the de-potted plants in potting soil.

8 Finally, fill the large shallow pan with nine sage plants (*Salvia farinacea* 'Rhea'). Use potting soil over pot shards. Space the plants so that the adult leaves will touch one another for a full display. Pinch out the tips of young shoots for a more bushy effect.

arranging the plants

See the photograph of the finished project on page 19. The taller plants create a backdrop of greenery for the colorful flowers in the foreground. For your own display you may wish to use steps or stages to create the right balance of height and bushiness.

masonry

Stone or marble containers, unless old, are difficult to find today, although they are still made in Italy to traditional designs. Cast concrete in various stone colors is more easily found. You can paint smooth surfaces in lime wash or distemper and allow more porous, pitted surfaces to acquire a patina naturally.

top Oriental glazed ceramic pots offer good value and are usually elegantly shaped. They are also available in blue and white, which looks good outdoors. Space them out on a terrace as a repeat element.

above A cast-concrete trough looks best patinated or distressed to complement the asters. Encourage moss and mold by painting with liquid fertilizer and keep in a damp, shaded position.

right A concrete basket-pattern pot of early 19th-century type echoes the basket-edged beds and actual basket planters often seen in Regency gardens. This sort of pot looks good raised on a low brick wall or wooden pier, displayed with pink geraniums.

far right This 1930s shaped urn, on account of its simple outline, makes a useful centerpiece that will hold its own against a complex background. It is planted for summer with blue solenopsis.

top Lightweight fiberglass reinforced concrete containers are useful for roof terraces or where containers need to be moved around. This one has been planted with a smoke bush.

above A shallow glazed ceramic bonsai trough makes a useful container for a low planting of eustoma. Keep shallow containers well watered because they are more susceptible than deeper ones to drying out.

above right An unadorned glazed ceramic container makes an attractive foil for a *Lavatera trimestris* 'Pink Beauty,' which is distinguished by its very pale pink flowers with purple veining and purple centers.

right This unusual pot has been cast to resemble an 18th-century water cistern and subsequently treated to look like lead. The pink of the hydrangeas is a good contrasting subject.

vertical planting

A good way to secure privacy in a town garden is to plant vertically. An ordinary hedge is one solution, but even on a roof terrace more interesting screening effects can be achieved using containers. This project shows how to get a banded effect of pleached linden underplanted with ivy, below which are containers for flowers. If you wish to enclose all the sides of your garden, simply add more troughs and trellis backing.

MATERIALS & EQUIPMENT

2 concrete (hypertufa) troughs 18 x 18 x 24 in (450 x 450 x 600 mm)

1 concrete (hypertufa) trough 18 x 18 x 18 in (450 x 450 x 450 mm)

dark green latex exterior paint

ready-made lattic panels, cut and framed in 1 x 2 in (25 x 50 mm) lumber to make a unit 6 x 6 ft (1.8 x 1.8 m)

2 pressure-treated posts 1½ x 1½ x 84 [2 x 2] (50 x 50 x 2200 mm)

coated wire or garden ties and sea-washed pebbles

pot shards, potting soil and slow-release fertilizer

1 red-twigged linden (*Tilia platyphyllos* 'Rubra')

6 ivy plants (*Hedera helix*)

8 white petunias

8 purple *Verbena tenera*

8 white trailing *Verbena tenuisecta* f. *alba*

1 Start by securing the trellis backing. In this project vertical posts have been attached to the outside of a 12 in (300 mm) high parapet. If you don't have a wall, secure the posts in the ground. Space them 6 ft (1.8 m) apart so that the trellis can be screwed to the face of the posts 12 in (300 mm) above ground level.

Alternatively, if you have a high wall or wooden fence, you can train your plants along wires. Stretch plastic or galvanized wire horizontally between vine eyes at suitable intervals and secure with screws.

2 Improve the appearance of the concrete troughs by painting them. Dark colors in matte finish work best with this planting plan.

3 For the square trough, choose a pot-grown linden with a dense root system and a straight stem, ideally about 6 ft (1.8 m) high with lateral branches at the top; plant in fall or early spring.

4 Cover the drainage holes with pot shards and line with soil. Ease the tree out of its pot and position it toward the back of the trough. Plant the ferns in front of the tree and work soil around the root balls, making sure they are level. Fill with soil to within 3 in (80 mm) of the top. Finally, add a top dressing of slow-release fertilizer and decorate the surface with pebbles.

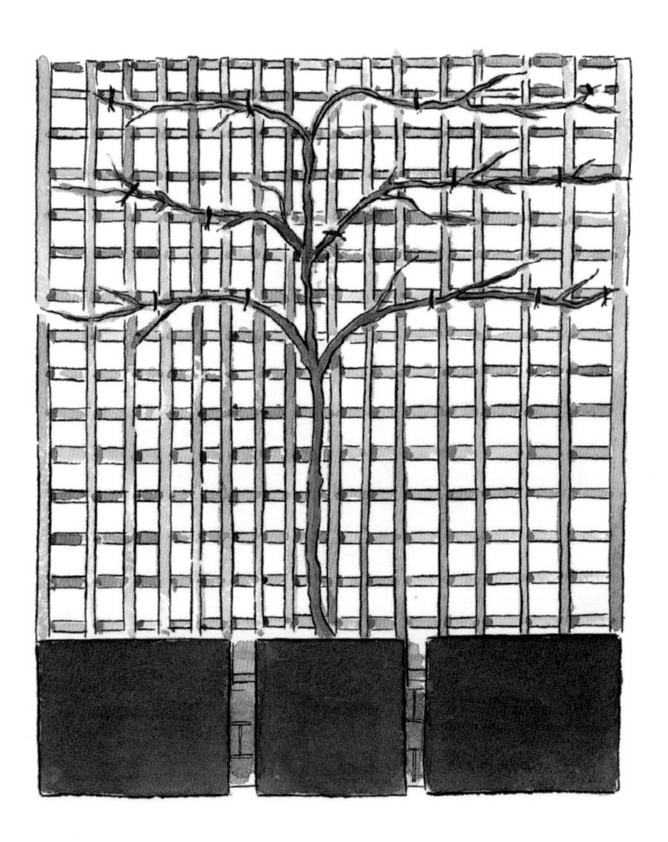

5 For the layered effect at the top of the trellis, three lines of lateral branches have been trained horizontally. Begin by choosing two strong laterals about 4 ft (1.2 m) from the base of the linden, on opposite sides of the stem. Secure them horizontally along the trellis with coated wire. Repeat for the next two lines, spacing them about 12 in (300 mm) apart.

6 Remove all the other side shoots from the stem and grow the trained laterals to the full width of the trellis. Prune annually and cut back excess foliage.

7 Line the larger troughs with pot shards and fill with soil to within 3 in (80 mm) of the top. Choose a plain green ivy with multiple stems that will provide a good hedgelike effect. Position three ivies at the back of each trough and top off with soil. To create a dense screen, train the ivy into a fan shape, tying it to the trellis with coated wire.

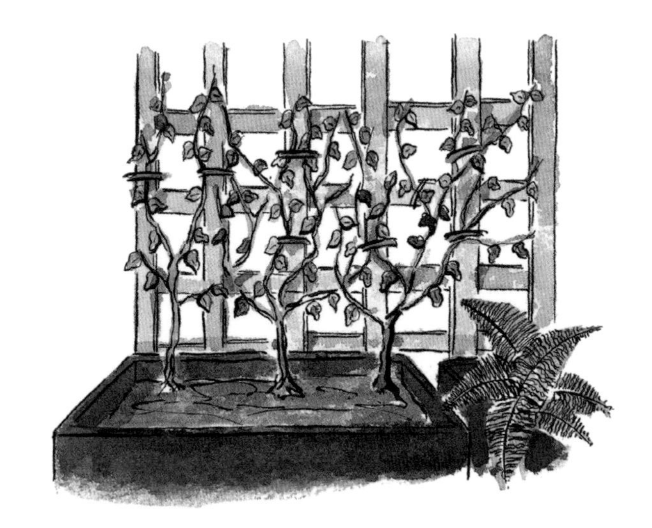

8 Grow the ivy to a height of 3 ft (900 mm) and allow the plants in both troughs to join together. Clip back to keep it flat against the trellis and maintain a straight line along the top; you don't want the ivy to meet the linden since this would make the layered effect less well defined.

9 Finish off the large troughs with a seasonal planting scheme. White petunias, purple verbenas, and white trailing verbenas have been planted along the front to give a long summer show. Keep well watered and fed. To make a longer wall screen or enclose a space, add to the number of troughs and secure additional lattice panels.

alternative planting plans

Plant forget-me-nots (*Myosotis alpestris*) for a blue haze in spring, or, for fall, plant orange or gold chysanthemums.

planting plans for urns

Urns are particularly popular in Italian gardens, where they form an integral part of the garden architecture. They can be used effectively to punctuate a design or, standing alone, to create a focal point; place them at intervals on walls and balustrades, or display them high on gate piers and plinths.

MATERIALS & EQUIPMENT

shallow "campagna"-shaped urn
pot shards
soil-based potting medium
plinth for display
10 houseleeks or hens-and-chicks (*Sempervivum tectorum*)
bear's breeches (*Acanthus mollis*)
Cordyline indivisa
lemon tree (*Citrus limon* 'Meyer')
trailing *Lobelia*

1 The shallow shape of a "campagna" urn complements the low-growing succulents used in this arrangement. Their shallow roots are not restricted by the container, making them an ideal choice.

Succulents need good drainage, so make sure there are holes in the base of the urn to prevent waterlogging. Place a layer of pot shards in the bottom of the container to improve drainage further.

2 Fill the urn with potting soil until it forms a dome-shaped mound above the rim. Thoroughly soak the soil.

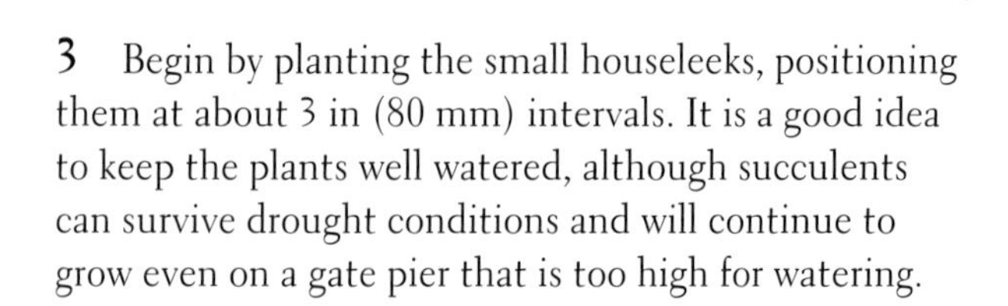

3 Begin by planting the small houseleeks, positioning them at about 3 in (80 mm) intervals. It is a good idea to keep the plants well watered, although succulents can survive drought conditions and will continue to grow even on a gate pier that is too high for watering.

4 As plants develop from the individual houseleeks, the surface will become covered, forming an unbroken mass. To enhance the display, allow the plants to spill over the edge on their aerial roots.

5 The sculpted effect produced by the sharp green leaves and tight rosettes looks best on a plinth; choose one of the same material as the urn or one of painted wood.

alternative planting plans

right A tall urn matches the proportions of the *Acanthus mollis* with its spikes of funnel-shaped flowers surrounded by deeply cut leaves.

above This Art Deco urn has been planted with trailing *Lobelia*. The profusion of pale blue flowers contrasts with the urn's clearly defined ridges.

left The size and shape of the Baroque urn suit a small lemon tree (*Citrus limon* 'Meyer'); the narrow neck helps the tree retain the moisture it needs.

above A large neoclassical urn has been chosen for the *Cordyline indivisa*, which needs room to spread.

a brickwork trough

A tall brick structure creates a stronger visual impact than could be achieved by an urn or a small planter. This trough provides the opportunity for a stunning display of flowering and non-flowering plants, which should nevertheless be simple enough to be appreciated from a distance. The trough can be used for a mixture of permanent structural planting and seasonal annuals—and will act as an important focal point in the garden all year around.

MATERIALS & EQUIPMENT

4 80 lb bags ready-to-mix concrete
3 80 lb bags ready-to-mix mortar
105 SW (frost-resistant) bricks, each 4 x 8 in (100 x 200 mm)
1 piece exterior-grade plywood ½ x 18 x 18 in (10 mm x 450 x 450)
4 concrete blocks (to set heights of planting platform)
30 quarts (30 liters) potting soil (approximately)
1 patio tree rose, such as *Rosa* 'Sanders' White Rambler'
1 *Hebe pinguifolia* 'Pagei'
18 tobacco plants (*Nicotiana alata* 'Lime Green')
brick chisel • concave jointer • level • mallet
mason's line • mason's trowel • stakes • wheelbarrow

1 The trough needs to be built onto 5 in (130 mm) foundations. Excavate a 28 in (700 mm) square hole to this depth. If your trough is to be sited on a gravel path, rake away the gravel from the area before digging the hole.

2 Add water to the ready-to-mix concrete—about two wheelbarrow loads of concrete are needed for the foundations.

3 Tip the concrete into the prepared hole, spreading it right into the corners. Level off with a straight-edged board and make sure there are no air pockets; use a spirit level to make sure the surface is horizontal. Leave to dry out for at least 24 hours, and preferably several days, using a plastic sheet to protect it from the weather.

4 Mark out 27 in (680 mm) square with string and pegs, 2½ in (65 mm) above the concrete bed, as a guide for the first course, or layer, of bricks.

5 Add water to the ready-to-mix mortar. Spread a layer of mortar ½ in (10 mm) thick on the concrete slab.

6 Position the bricks as shown. Lay the first course with the "frog" (a small indentation) at the top, spreading all brick ends with mortar. Lay the second layer staggered over the joints on the first. After this and later courses, remove excess mortar from joints.

7 When the mortar is thick enough to hold a thumbprint, run a concave jointer over the joints.

8 Continue to build the container until it has nine layers of brick; make sure the face and height are even by checking at regular intervals with a level.

9 Complete the trough with a coping course, stepping out the brick by 1 in (25 mm). Four filler pieces about 2 x 4 in (50 x 100 mm) are needed to stretch the coping over the edges. (Make odd-sized pieces by scoring the brick all around with a brick chisel and mallet; hit the scored area with increasing intensity until the brick splits.) Fill the inside corners of the step with concrete.

11 To avoid having to fill the entire container with soil, make a stage from the plywood. First drill five 1 in (25 mm) diameter holes in the wood for drainage. Then place the four concrete blocks inside the structure and rest the plywood over them.

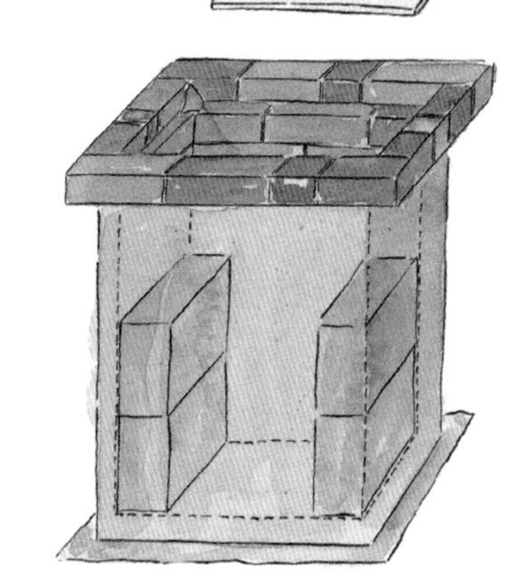

12 For the following planting plan, the hebes and tree rose remain in their plastic pots but are set in soil, whereas the tobacco plants are planted directly into the soil.

13 Place the rose in the center, below the level of the top of the container, then add enough soil to sit the hebes flush with the coping layer. Fill in the spaces with soil, placing the tobacco plants around the rose. Keep the display well watered; use a liquid fertilizer each week.

alternative planting plans

The planting can change with the season. For winter, consider a half-standard holly (*Ilex* x *meserveae* 'Blue Prince') with Kew wintercreeper (*Euonymous fortunei Kewensis*); for fall, try chysanthemums and flowering kale; for spring, a boxwood cone (*Buxus sempervirens*) surrounded by blue hyacinths.

a circular pipe with flowering tree

In a paved garden or in a place where soil is not available, large shrubs or small trees can be grown in broad concrete pipes—an inexpensive solution for containing soil and displaying plants. Here a decorative niche gives height to the arrangement and frames the cascading flowers of the fuchsia plant with its frothy mass of underplanting.

MATERIALS & EQUIPMENT

1 section of concrete drainage pipe 20 in (500 mm) high with a 36 in (900 mm) diameter

exterior-grade paint (that can be used on concrete) dark blue-green

50 quarts (50 liters) potting soil (approximately)

slow-release fertilizer

pot shards or coarse gravel

1 standard weeping *Fuchsia* x *speciosa* 'La Bianca'

10 lady's mantle (*Alchemilla mollis*)

6 geranium (*P.* 'Friesdorf')

1 Choose a concrete drainage pipe to fit the size of the plant. The dimensions given on page 36 are suitable for a small to medium shrub. Conceal the rough surface of the pipe with a fresh coat of paint; dark blue-green harmonizes with most garden schemes.

2 Place the painted pipe in your garden on a level patch of ground. If you plan to use a fuchsia, choose a spot that is relatively shady. Fill the base of the pipe to a depth of 1–2 in (30–50 mm) with pot shards; this will help improve drainage.

3 Carefully take the fuchsia out of the pot and tease out any enmeshed roots. Fill the base of the pipe with enough soil to cover the pot shards and add granular fertilizer. When you have finished planting, all of the plants should be at the depth they were in the pots (see illustration).

4 Add moistened potting soil to bring the plants and soil to a level about $1\frac{1}{2}$ in (40 mm) below the rim of the pipe.

5 Position the fuchsia in the center of the pipe. Again, the soil surface should be about $1\frac{1}{2}$ in (40 mm) from the top of the pipe.

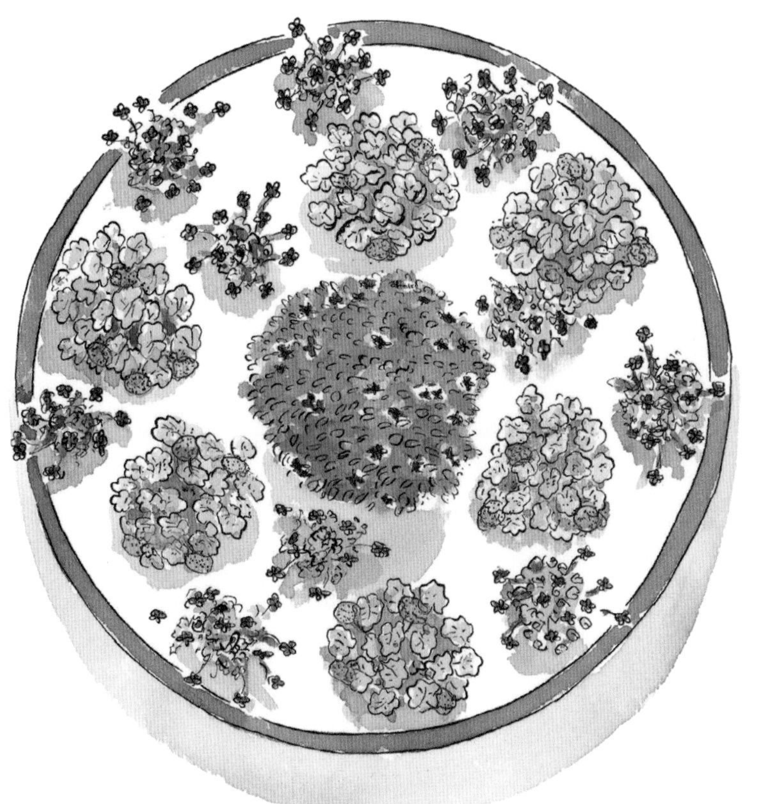

6 Underplant with lady's mantle and geraniums, and place them around the edge of the container in the positions shown in the illustration.

7 Pack the soil firmly around all the plants and water thoroughly. Monitor the planter for moisture, especially during hot weather.

alternative planting plan

Use two pipes of different diameters to achieve a stepped effect—an idea inspired by medieval garden designs. Plant your tree in the central pipe and fill in the lower level with a seasonal planting scheme. This alternative planting display uses a weeping mulberry (*Morus alba* 'Pendula') above a bed of chamomile (*Anthemis nobile* 'Treneague').

a shell-faced trough

A simple decorative treatment refines the look of a concrete garden trough. Aluminium leaf adds a shiny surface to the shells but any metal leaf works well—the most extravagant-looking option being gold. Blue tones have been chosen for the planting arrangement since they complement the silvery-gray of the trough and shells. If you pick your own display, try to stick to one color—a mixture may detract from the decorative impact of the container.

MATERIALS & EQUIPMENT

plain concrete (hypertufa) trough 10 x 24 in (250 x 600)
5 large scallop shells
1 quart (1 liter) dark gray primer
5 sheets metal leaf (with adhesive)
paintbrush
two-part epoxy glue
30 quarts (30 liters) potting soil (approximately)
pot shards
pot-grown plants in 3–4 in (80–100 mm) pots, as follows:
5 *Delphinium belladonna* 'Wendy'
3 Cherry-pie heliotrope (*Heliotropium peruvianum* 'Royal Marine')
5 *Laurentia axillaris* 'Blue Star'
5 *Aptenia cordifolia* 'Variegata'

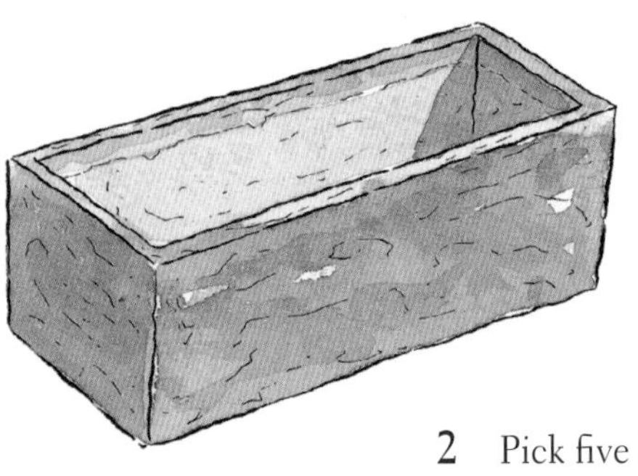

1 Paint the four sides of the trough and the first 1 in (25 mm) inside the top edge with the primer.

2 Pick five large scallop shells of roughly the same size; these can be purchased at a fish market or a craft store. Clean and dry them thoroughly before applying the treatment. Paint the convex side with a single coat of primer.

3 When the primer on the shells has dried, apply the adhesive for the metal leaf (follow manufacturer's instructions).

4 Apply the transfer leaf over the tacky surface of a shell; test that the adhesive is ready by placing a corner of the transfer onto the shell; if it instantly adheres, the shell is ready to take the leaf.

5 Attach the leaf to the rest of the shell and rub it down lightly with cotton wool. To achieve a distressed appearance, adhere the leaf to the raised areas of the shell; to do this, stretch the transfer over the upper surface and rub the top ridges only so that when you remove the backing the leaf has not stuck in the indents. Repeat this treatment for all five shells.

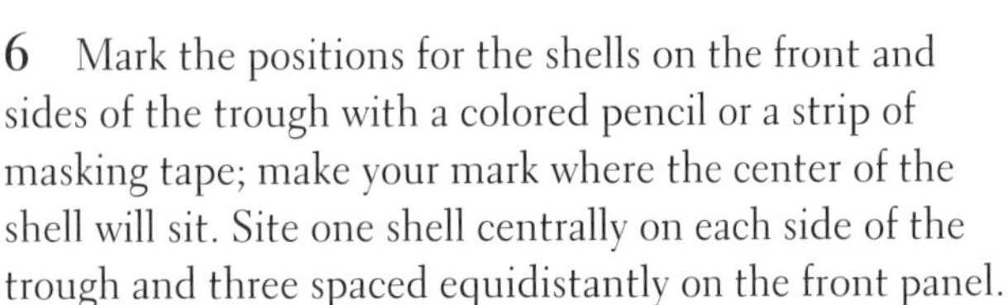

6 Mark the positions for the shells on the front and sides of the trough with a colored pencil or a strip of masking tape; make your mark where the center of the shell will sit. Site one shell centrally on each side of the trough and three spaced equidistantly on the front panel.

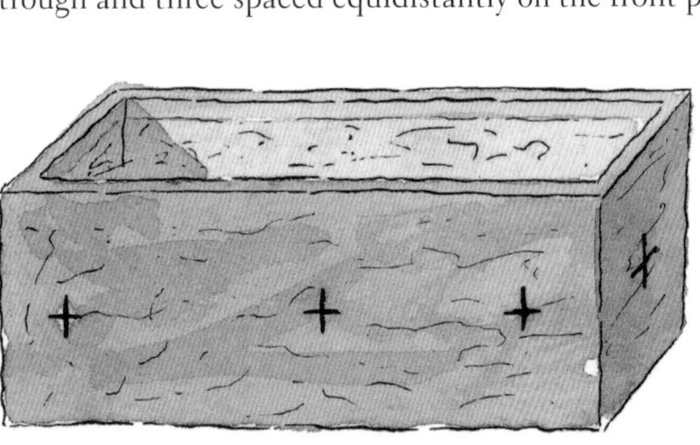

7 The trough and shells are now ready to be joined together. Mix the epoxy glue. Using the applicator or a small wooden spatula, apply generous blobs of the glue to the inside edges of the shells in four or five places, as shown.

8 Tip the trough onto its side so that the front face is pointing up. Press each shell onto the three marked positions along the top and remove any excess glue spilling out from the sides with a clean applicator.

9 When the glue has dried, turn the trough back onto its base and affix the side shells; hold these in position while the glue sets.

10 Put the trough in a sunny location and plant it in June, using the plan on the left as a guide. The plants have been placed in rows and staggered to fit. The delphiniums are along the back, followed by the laurentias; the heliotropes and the aptenias are at the front.

11 Cover the drainage holes with pot shards. Take the plants out of their pots and tease out the roots. Add moistened potting soil until the plants and the surrounding soil are about 1 in (25 mm) from the trough's rim.

alternative planting plans

For spring, plant *Convolvulus sabatius* with *Vinca minor* 'Alba Variegata'; in winter, fill the trough with winter-flowering pansies.

metal

Lead is one of the most beautiful metals and acquires a natural patina if left outdoors. (Attaching sheet lead to a wood frame is much cheaper than using solid cast lead.) Cast iron can look attractive if left to rust, but it is usually painted—dark colors tend to be more effective than light ones; before applying any paint to cast iron, it is important to prime the surface against corrosion. Galvanized steel or wirework is another finish that can be used to create decorative effects in outdoor plantings; it can either be painted or left in its original grayish-silver reflective state. If you want to add a touch of glitter to a metal container, apply a gold-leaf or silver-leaf detail.

right A 19th-century-style wirework stand proves useful for displaying a seasonally changing mix of plants in terra-cotta pots. Ferns combine well with white annuals. Paint wirework a color that will show up against its background—here a dark color has been used to read against a pale blue wall.

below A tall galvanized pot is shown off to best advantage by seasonal planting in a raised plastic liner. Lilies have been chosen for a late spring to early summer planting—their architectural lines complement the slender, upright shape of this particular container.

above This shallow wirework basket is overflowing with coleus—the tender foliage plant that was loved by the Victorians for its rich, rather artificial-looking variegated colors, reminiscent of the damasks of the period.

above right A deep galvanized potato picker painted in dark green high-gloss paint makes an attractive jardinière for larger seasonally changed plants. Here it has been planted up with yellow *Lilium* 'Reinesse'—leave the lilies in their plastic pots so that they can easily be changed at the end of the flowering season.

right These osteospermums in a shallow galvanized tub will have a long summer flowering season. They are now available in a wide color range and with different petal shapes.

top A tall "campagna"-shaped urn can take a taller mass of planting than the shallower type of urn. From summer through to early fall, dahlias provide a colorful display reminiscent of the late 19th century.

above Herbs can frequently be grown to eye-catching decorative effect in containers. In this case, a prostrate rosemary has been planted in an ornate metal goblet. The herb's curving branches and tiny pale blue flowers are in perfect harmony with the swirls on the cup.

a wirework basket

This unusual wire framework was inspired by similar edgings used in the early 19th century as plant supports. A galvanized-metal strip at the bottom creates a border around a basketlike stand that acts as an attractive frame for rambling rose bushes. The metal should be think enough to cut with tin cutters. The best roses to use for this project are low-growing groundcover types, but you can adapt the basket to accommodate any size of plant, such as larger shrub roses.

MATERIALS & EQUIPMENT

2 pieces galvanized sheet metal 4 x 48 in (100 x 1200 mm)
1 piece galvanized sheet metal 4 x 24 in (100 x 600 mm)
(use a gauge that can be cut with tin cutters)
6 galvanized roofing bolts 1/2 in (10 mm) long and 1/4 in (6 mm) wide
72 ft (22 m) of galvanized fencing wire about 3/16 in (5 mm) thick
1 piece plywood 1 x 14 x 21 in (25 x 350 x 525 mm)
small pot gray-blue metal primer
roll of thin galvanized wire
well-rotted manure and rose fertilizer
5 bare-root roses such as *Rosa* 'The Fairy'
hacksaw • mallet • sabersaw • tin cutters • vise or C-clamp

1 Drill two 3/8 in (7 mm) diameter holes at the ends of each galvanized-metal strip. Then connect the three sections together to form a ring by lining up the holes at the ends and securing the joins with roofing bolts through the prepared holes. This strip acts as a template for preparing the bed and as a retainer for the basket.

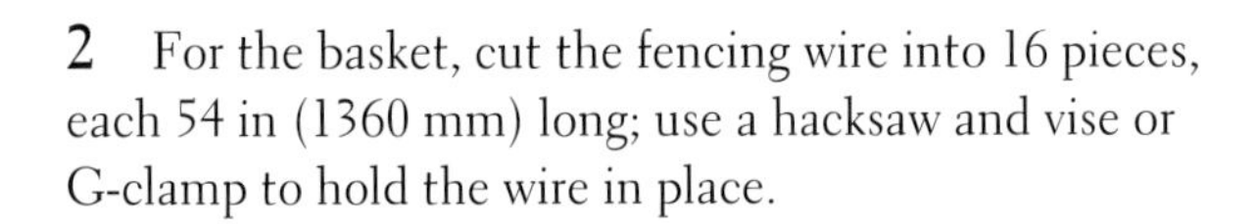

2 For the basket, cut the fencing wire into 16 pieces, each 54 in (1360 mm) long; use a hacksaw and vise or G-clamp to hold the wire in place.

3 To shape the wire, you need to make a template from the plywood; this will act as a solid pattern around which to bend your wire. Mark the center point at the top and draw the curved sides to within 8 in (200 mm) of the bottom; this section of the arch remains straight. Cut out the shape with a sabersaw.

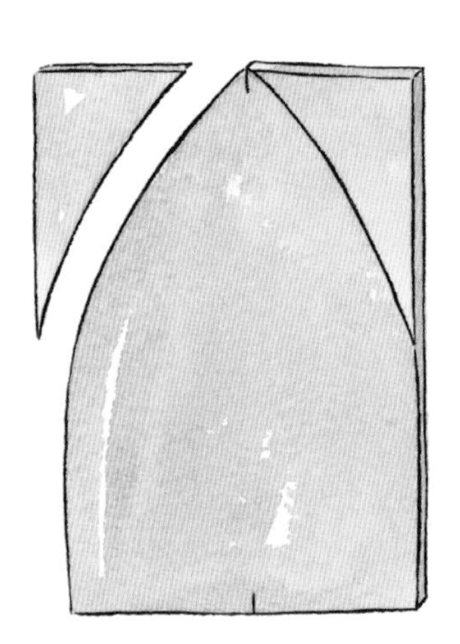

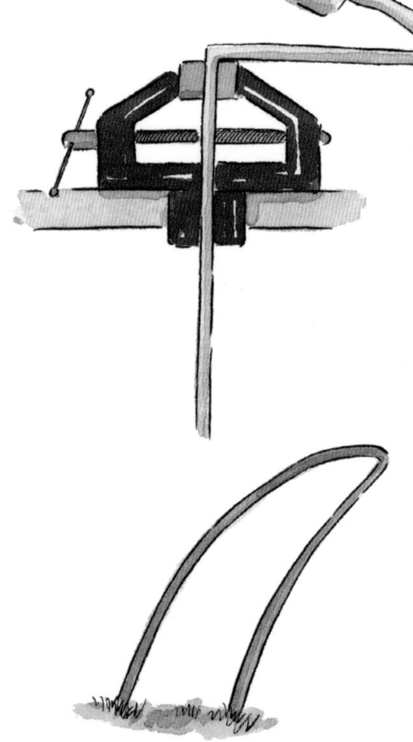

4 Mark the center point on each length of fencing wire. Using a vise, bend the wire at this point into a right angle; it helps to use a mallet as well.

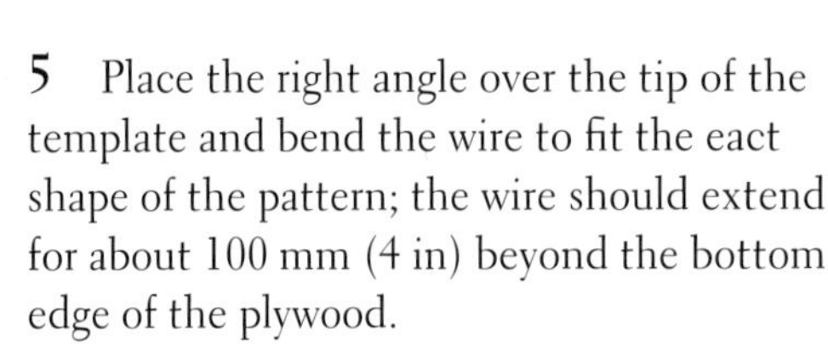

5 Place the right angle over the tip of the template and bend the wire to fit the eact shape of the pattern; the wire should extend for about 100 mm (4 in) beyond the bottom edge of the plywood.

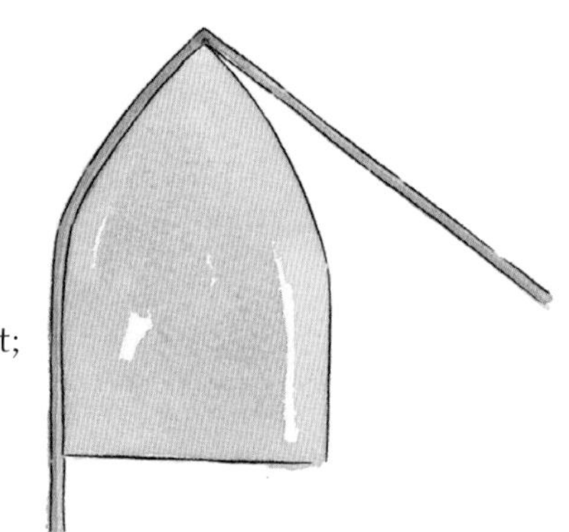

6 Each section of the frame needs to be bent out; turn the arches sideways and use the template to check the curves are all the same.

7 Before constructing the basket shape, paint all the metal components with the metal primer; the gray-blue used here looks like a copper patina and provides a good foil for the pink roses.

8 Choose a sunny, flat site for your rose bed. If the area is covered with grass, position the ring and cut around its inner edge to mark the turf. Put the ring to one side and remove the turf by dividing it into squares and lifting out with a spade.

9 Till the bed thorougly, adding well-rotted manure; gently press the ring in position.

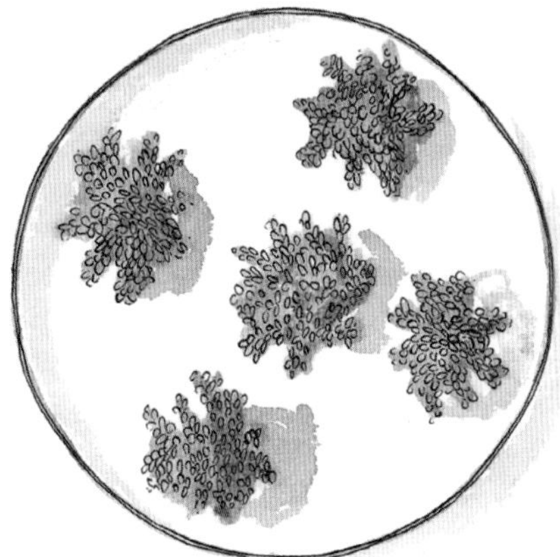

10 Plant the five roses, positioning them according to the planting plan shown on the left. Make sure that the junctions of stem and root are at surface level. Top dress with rose fertilizer.

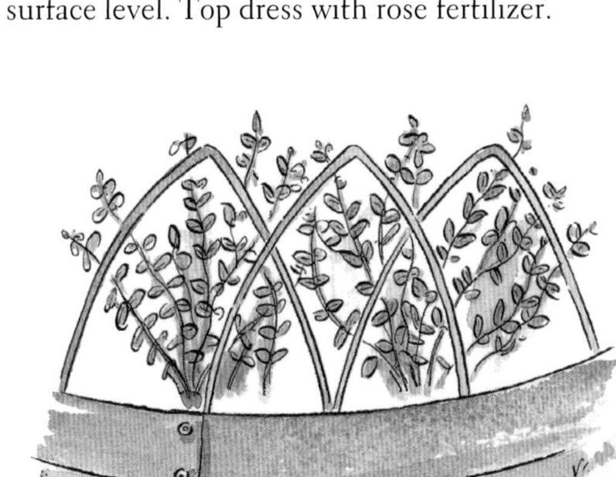

11 Insert the first arch hard up against the inner edge of the ring with the tip bending out and push it about 6–8 in (150–200 mm) into the ground. Insert the next arch so that it overlaps the original one by half its width. Repeat this process for the remaining arches all the way around the circumference; you may need to readjust the spacing on some of the arches for a neat and even fit.

12 Secure the basket sections together by twisting the galvanized wire around the intersections on each arch.

13 Prune the roses so that they form a slightly domed shape and trim any grass around the outer edge for a formal effect.

alternative planting plans

Try the roses 'White Pet' or 'Nozomi' for a container of this size; for a larger arrangement, use the pink rose 'Marguerite Hilling' or its creamy white sister 'Nevada.' A suitable shrub would be *Camellia japonica* 'Alba Plena.'

galvanized buckets

Hanging galvanized buckets on "S" hooks is an inexpensive and attractive way of displaying plants. A bright and vibrant arrangement, such as the one used here, adds a splash of color, decoration, and movement to a blank expanse of wall in a simple setting. Choose similar flowers in sharp colors and bold shapes to contrast with the plain outline and shiny silver-gray surface of the buckets. For quick results, buy plants instead of starting from seed.

MATERIALS & EQUIPMENT

3 galvanized buckets 12 in (300 mm) in diameter

3 substantial galvanized angle brackets with tops 8½ in (220 mm) long and sides 10 in (250 mm) long

3 eye bolts with nuts to fit the holes in the angle brackets

3 "S" hooks 3 in (80 mm) long

no. 10 plated screws 2 in (50 mm)

pot shards

15 quarts (15 liters) potting soil (approximately)

4 African marigold (*Tagetes erecta*)

2 pot marigold (*Calendula officinalis*)

2 *Artemisia* 'Powys Castle'

2 marguerite (*Argyranthemum frutescens*)

2 black-eyed Susan (*Rudbeckia hirta*)

1 To prepare the buckets for planting, drill three drainage holes in the base of each one.

2 Line the bottom of each bucket with a layer of pot shards 1 in (25 mm) thick.

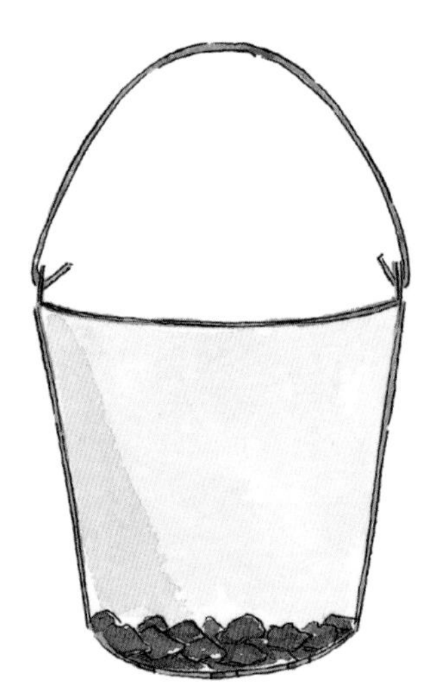

3 Fill the buckets about two-thirds of the way up with moistened potting soil. Place four de-potted plants in each, making sure that the root ball is 1 in (25 mm) below the top edge of the bucket. Fill in with soil around the edges, lightly covering the surface of the root balls, and pack the soil. Give the plants a good soaking.

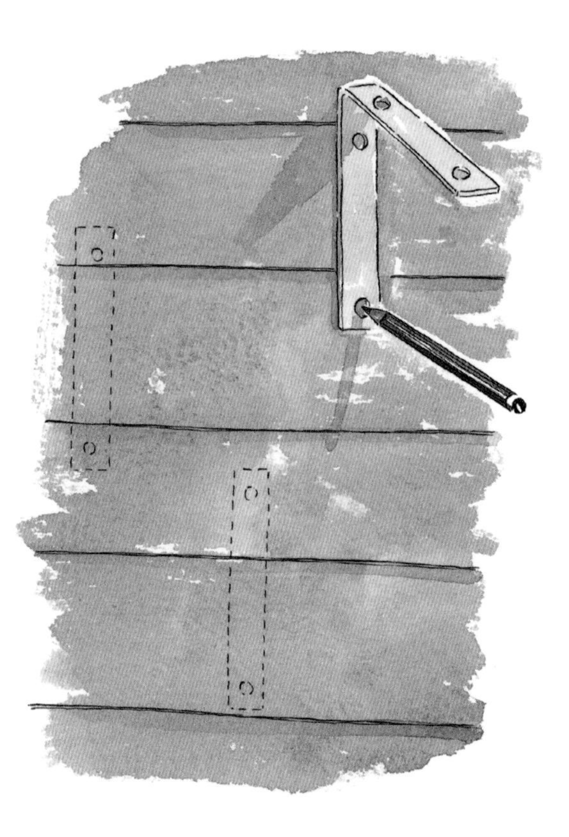

4 The plants used in this project need plenty of sun, so make sure your display area is in a sunny spot—a south-facing wall is ideal. Mark the position of each bracket on the wall with a pencil. In the example shown, the brackets have been staggered up a wall to allow enough space for plants to spread.

To attach the brackets to a stone wall, follow step 5. To attach the brackets to wood, follow step 6.

5 Use a power drill, a masonry bit, and special masonry screws to attach the brackets to brick or stone.

6 For wood surfaces use no. 10 screws. If possible, attach the screws into a stud.

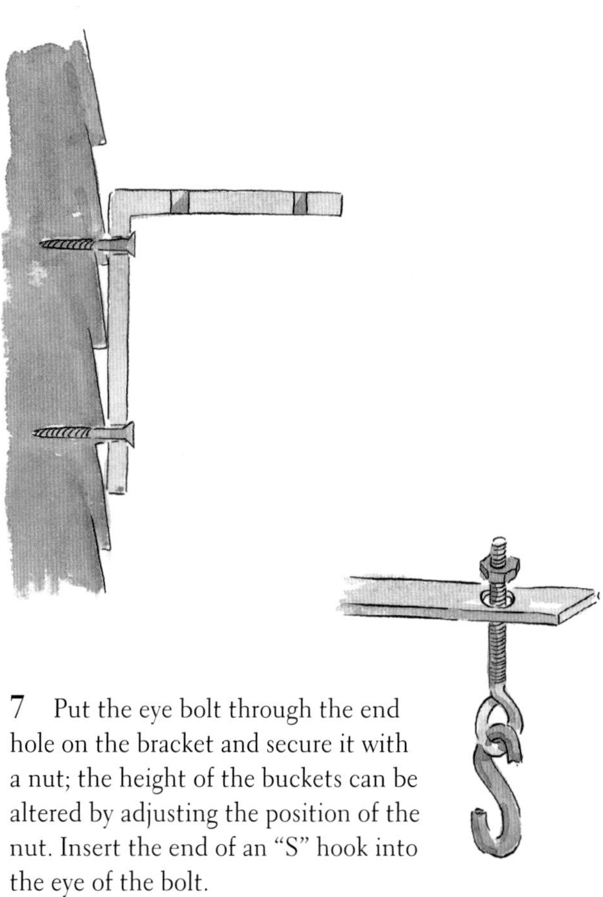

7 Put the eye bolt through the end hole on the bracket and secure it with a nut; the height of the buckets can be altered by adjusting the position of the nut. Insert the end of an "S" hook into the eye of the bolt.

8 This bucket has been planted with marguerites and black-eyed Susans. It is especially important to keep all the plants well watered because the containers dry out quickly. Check daily if possible.

alternative planting plan

Bring a burst of sunshine to a bare wall by filling your buckets with dwarf sunflowers (*Helianthus*), *Coreopsis tinctoria*, and *Gazania* 'Orange Beauty.'

a lead-faced trough

Lead patinates to a beautiful silvery-gray color—an effect that is simple and quick to achieve. You can simulate the appearance of a lead container by fixing sheet lead to a wooden framework. Take care over size and placement; a window box must sit within the frame and be secured on brackets. Before embarking on this project, ensure that this style of container is in sympathy with the character and architecture of your building.

MATERIALS & EQUIPMENT

wooden box 8 x 8 x 36 in (230 x 250 x 950 mm)

2 pieces softwood $\frac{3}{4}$ x 1$\frac{1}{2}$ x 9$\frac{1}{2}$ in [1 x 2] (30 x 30 x 285 mm)

1 piece softwood $\frac{3}{4}$ x 1$\frac{1}{2}$ x 39 in [1 x 2] (30 x 30 x 1030 mm)

no. 8 screws 1$\frac{1}{2}$ in (40 mm)

galvanized nails $\frac{3}{4}$ in (20 mm)

1 quart (1 liter) exterior-grade wood preservative and 1 bottle white vinegar

2 sheets of $\frac{1}{24}$ in lead (or 26-gauge galvanized sheet metal),
one 8 x 52 in (250 x 1430 mm) and the other 5 x 58 in (130 x 1550)

6 *Senecio cineraria*

5 *Petunia* 'Ruby'

4 *Osteospermum* 'Whirly Gig'

3 pink bellflower (*Campanula carpatica*)

3 *Nemesia caerulea*

3 Persian violet (*Exacum affine*)

1 Treat the box inside and out with wood preservative. Wear gloves and and wash your hands when handling the lead, and cut it with tin cutters.

2 Attach the wider strip of lead to one side of the box, top and bottom, with the galvanized nails.

3 Wrap the lead around to the front and use a mallet to achieve a sharp corner.

4 Nail the front in place, top and bottom, at 5–6 in (100–150 mm) intervals. Use the mallet on the other corner and nail the remaining side in place.

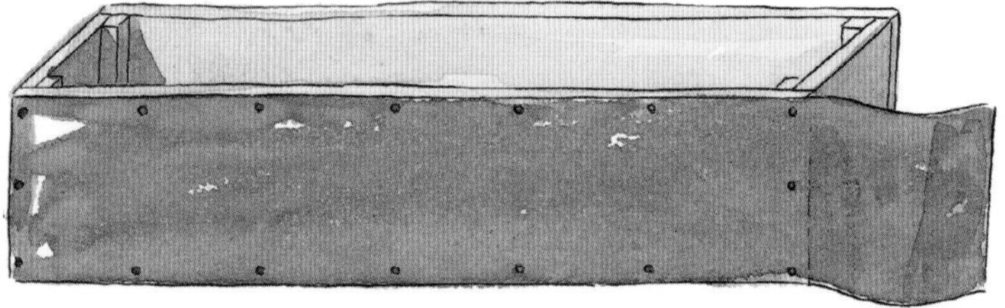

5 Take the three sections of softwood and miter one corner on the short pieces and both corners on the longer one. Fit the sections together to form the molding around the front and sides of the box, flush with the top edge. Drill holes for the screws around this edge and screw the moulding in place from the inside.

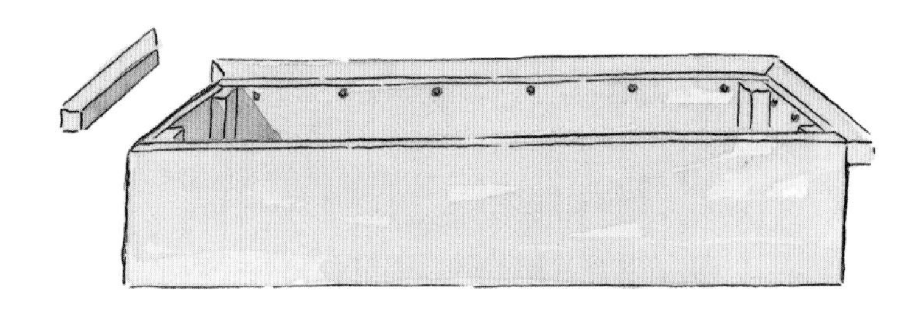

6 Take the second strip of lead and score a line along its length, using a nail and straight edge, 2¼ in (60 mm) down from the top. Divide the bottom into 31 sections of 2 in (50 mm), then divide the scored line into sections of the same size but starting 1 in (25 mm) in from the short end.

7 Join up the marks to form a zigzag pattern and then cut it out using tin cutters.

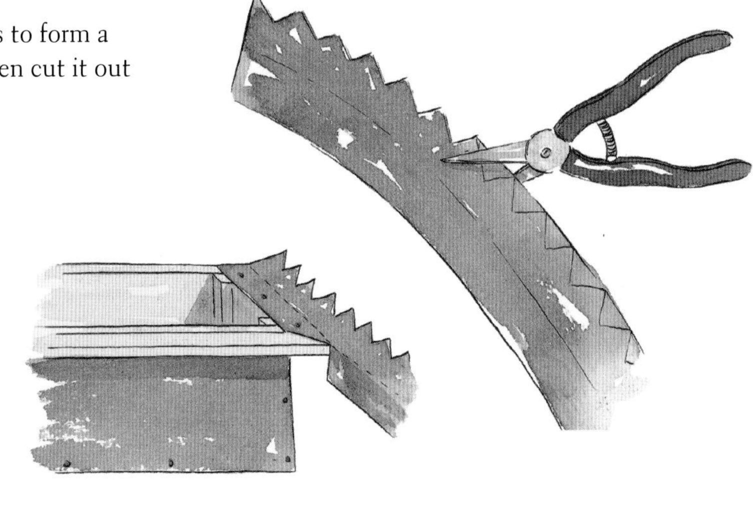

8 Place the straight edge of the cutout along the inner edge of the box on the side. Nail it in place.

9 To attach the strip neatly around the corner cut out a 90° notch from the lead, making sure the corner point lines up exactly with the corner of the moulding. Hammer down the zigzag edge on the side and wrap the lead to the front of the box.

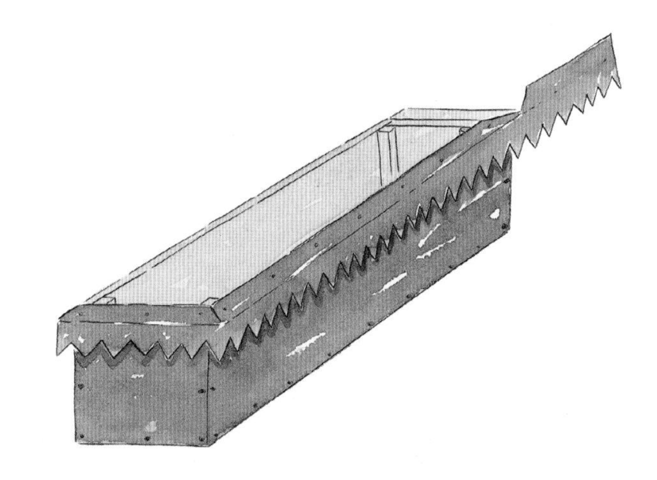

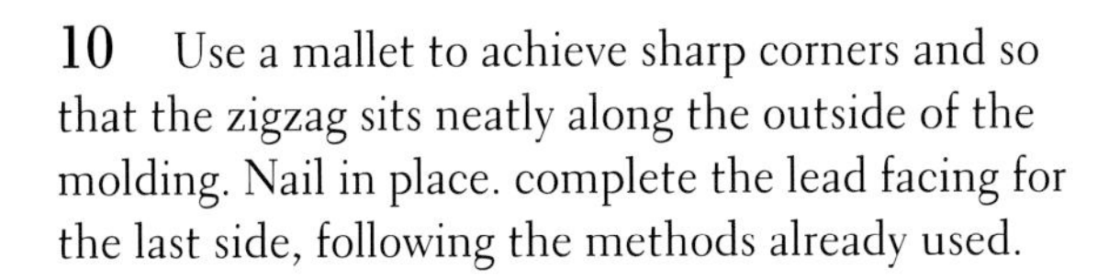

10 Use a mallet to achieve sharp corners and so that the zigzag sits neatly along the outside of the molding. Nail in place. complete the lead facing for the last side, following the methods already used.

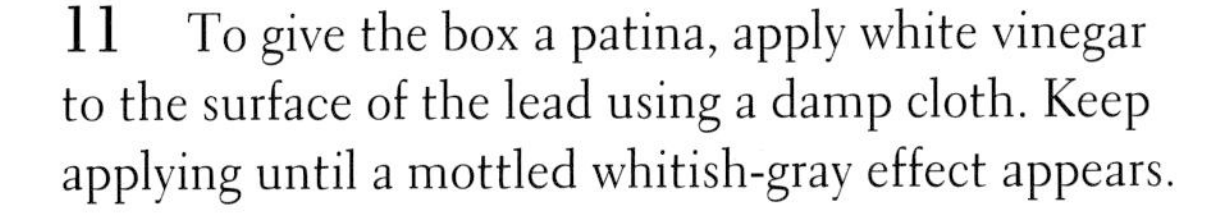

11 To give the box a patina, apply white vinegar to the surface of the lead using a damp cloth. Keep applying until a mottled whitish-gray effect appears.

12 If your window sill slopes, make wedges to level the base of the box. Secure by screwing the inside of the box to the window frame or use ready-made window-box brackets.

13 Line the box with pot shards and moistened potting soil. Add the plants, matching the colors and numbers listed on page 54 with the plan below. Fill in with potting soil to 1 in (25 mm) below the top, pack it down and water thoroughly

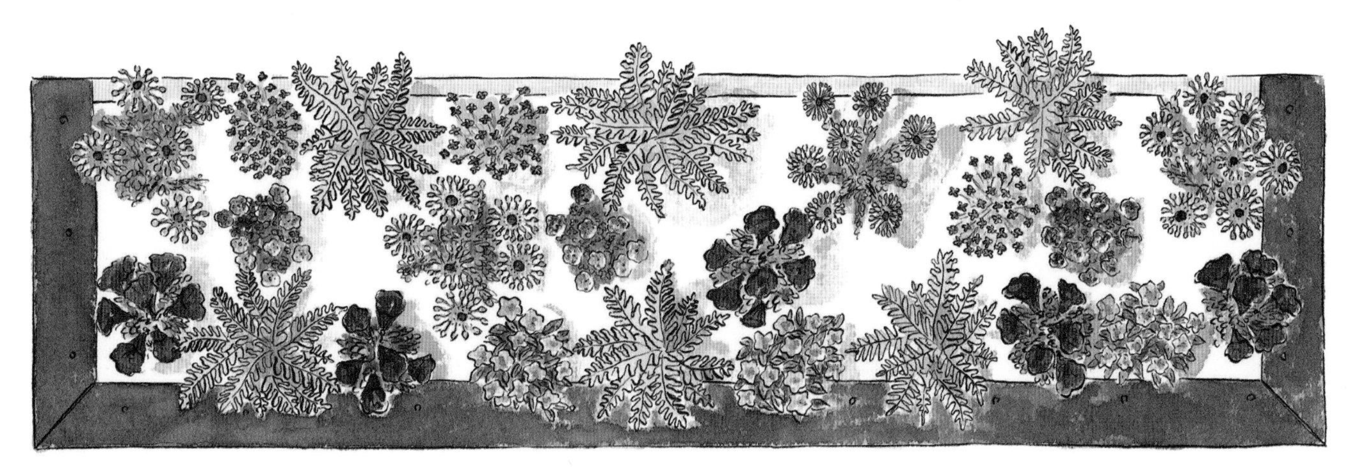

a wirework hanging basket

A 19th-century wirework basket makes an attractive hanging display. This one is particularly large, making it all the more striking. Anything larger would be impractical on account of the weight of the plants and soil. Site it on its own between an upstairs window and a door, or place one either side of a front door as a welcoming display.

MATERIALS & EQUIPMENT

wirework basket 24 in (600 mm) in diameter
no. 10 Phillips plated screws 1½ in (40 mm) and wall anchors
galvanized angle bracket with top 14 in (350 mm) long
threaded eye bolt with nuts to fit angle bracket and large "S" hook
peat- or fiber-based lightweight potting medium and sphagnum moss
pot-grown plants in 3 in (80 mm) plastic pots as follows:
10 *Petunia surfina*
5 *Fuchsia* 'Margaret'
5 geraniums (*Pelargonium* 'Balcon Royale')
6 *Petunia* 'Express Ruby'
6 heliotropes (*Heliotropium peruvianum*)
6 tobacco plants (*Nicotiana* 'Domino Pink')

1 You can buy decorative cast-iron shelf brackets, but for an elaborate basket such as this one it is better to use a plain bracket painted to match the wall surface.

Attach the bracket to the wall using Phillips screws and wall anchors. When choosing a position, consider ease of hanging and watering, and when attaching make sure the bracket is firmly in place, particularly when displaying over a path or doorway.

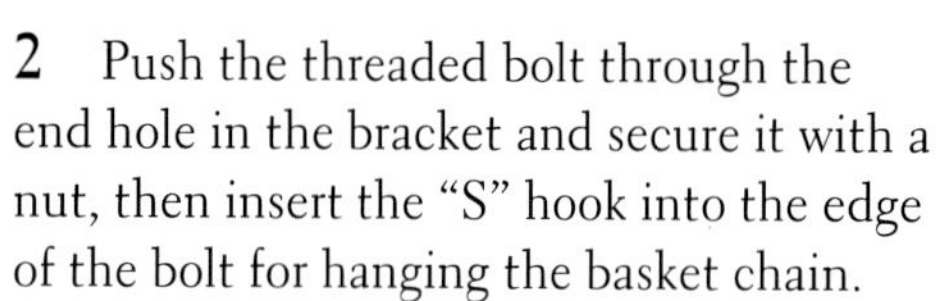

2 Push the threaded bolt through the end hole in the bracket and secure it with a nut, then insert the "S" hook into the edge of the bolt for hanging the basket chain.

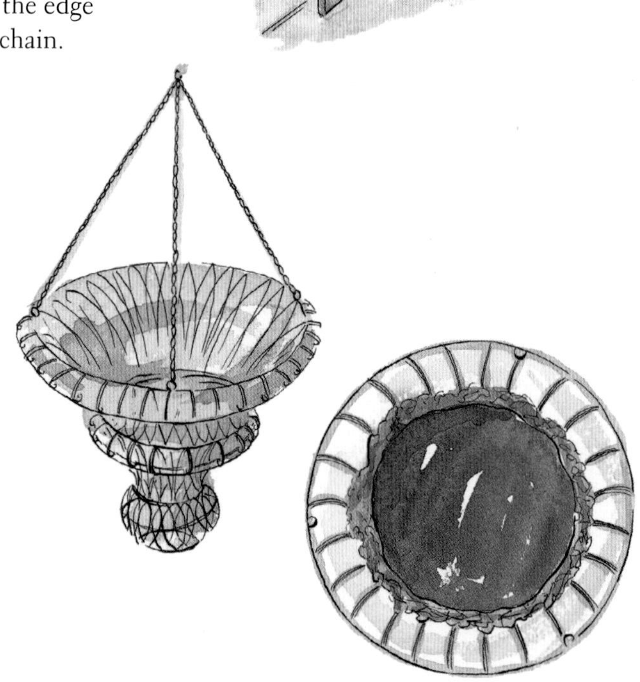

3 It is easier to work on the basket if you place it in a bucket—or hang it on a rope from a garage or shed door lintel or between a pair of folding steps.

4 Start by pushing the moss into the bottom of the container to a thickness of 1 in (25 mm) and place a layer of soil over it to keep it in place. Continue lining the basket with moss, filling it with soil as you go, until the frame has been covered up to the top edge.

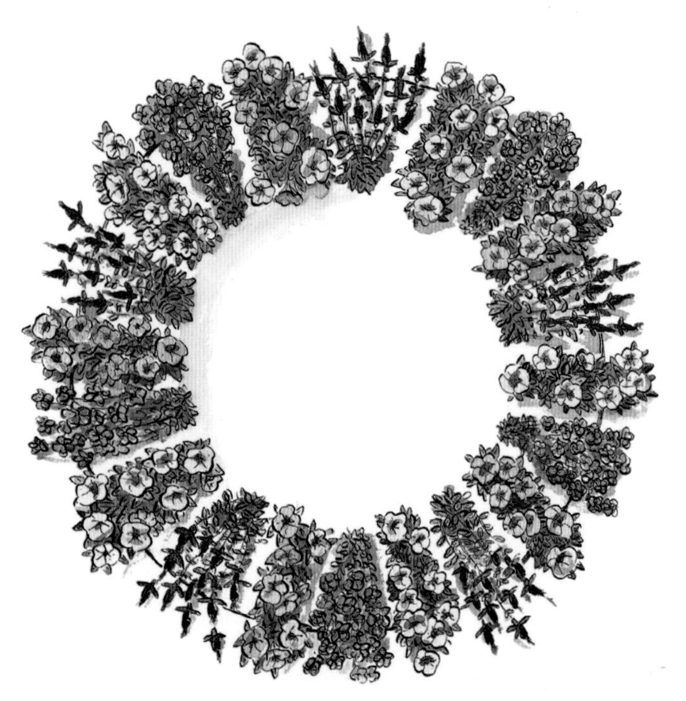

5 The plants used here are for a summer display; plant in late May. Start with the trailing plants around the edge: the ten petunias, the fuchsias, and the geraniums. Position them according to the plan; lean them slightly outward to follow the angle of the basket; keep them close together but with a thin layer of soil between each and around the outside edge.

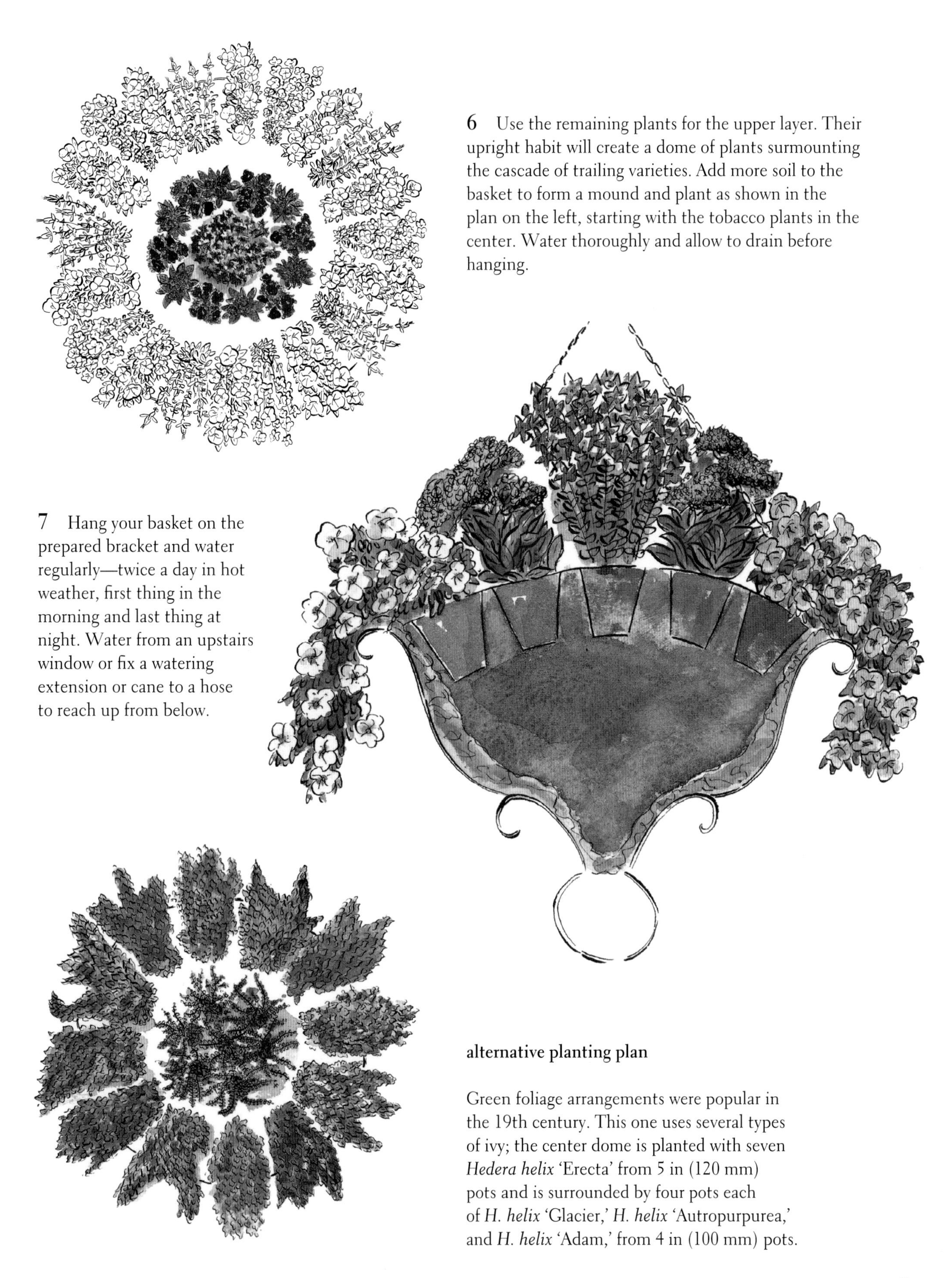

6 Use the remaining plants for the upper layer. Their upright habit will create a dome of plants surmounting the cascade of trailing varieties. Add more soil to the basket to form a mound and plant as shown in the plan on the left, starting with the tobacco plants in the center. Water thoroughly and allow to drain before hanging.

7 Hang your basket on the prepared bracket and water regularly—twice a day in hot weather, first thing in the morning and last thing at night. Water from an upstairs window or fix a watering extension or cane to a hose to reach up from below.

alternative planting plan

Green foliage arrangements were popular in the 19th century. This one uses several types of ivy; the center dome is planted with seven *Hedera helix* 'Erecta' from 5 in (120 mm) pots and is surrounded by four pots each of *H. helix* 'Glacier,' *H. helix* 'Autropurpurea,' and *H. helix* 'Adam,' from 4 in (100 mm) pots.

a painted galvanized washtub

A galvanized tin or enamel bath can be turned into an elegant planter by adding ball feet to give it the look of an early 19th-century jardinière. This planter is good for a large mass of colorful annuals and looks attractive on the ground or raised on a low plinth or wall. Paint it to complement the colors of your plants and surroundings.

MATERIALS & EQUIPMENT

oval washtub 24 in (600 mm) long and 18 in (450 mm) wide
1 piece exterior-grade plywood 3/4 x 14 x 18 in (18 x 350 x 450 mm)
4 wooden balls with 2 1/2 in (65 mm) diameter
4 dowels 2 in (50 mm) long with 3/8 in (7 mm) diameter
waterproof carpenter's glue
small jar Japan goldsize
1 packet or twelve 2 x 2 in (50 x 50 mm) squares gold leaf (with adhesive)
1 pint (1/2 liter) each clear wood preservative and dark red primer
1 quart (1 liter) paint (optional)
30 quarts (30 liters) potting soil (approximately)
bag of sphagnum moss
36 dwarf pink and red flowering tobacco plants (*Nicotiana* Domino Series)

1 Begin by making a plywood base to fit in the recessed stand underneath the tub; the ball feet will be attached to this. Place the tub on the plywood and mark the shape of the base on the plywood with a pencil.

2 Draw a second oval about 1/4 in (5 mm) inside the first. Cut out the inner shape using a sabersaw.

3 Drill a 3/8 in (7 mm) diameter hole about halfway through each of the wooden balls, making sure it is straight and centered.

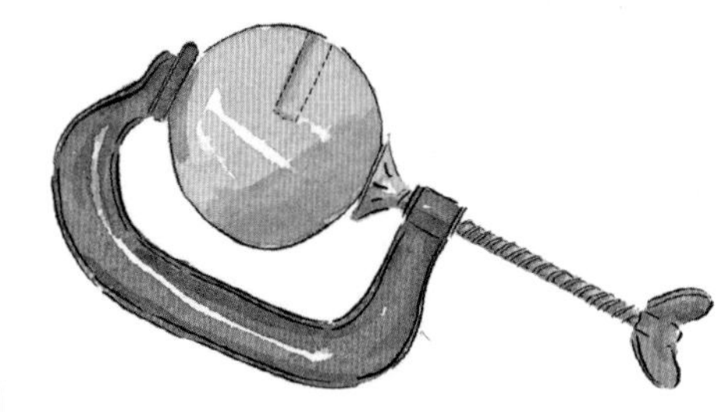

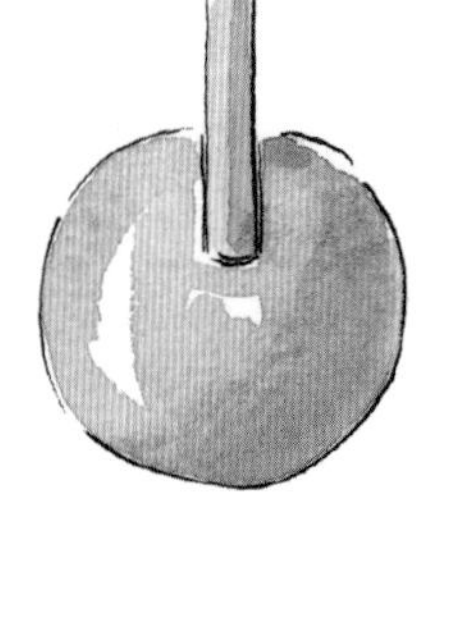

4 Dribble a little glue inside these holes and insert the dowels so that they stick out about 1 in (25 mm) above the surface of the balls.

5 Paint the feet with wood preservative. When that has dried, apply two coats of dark red primer to simulate the color of red gesso, which will give the finished effect a warm glow. Sand between each coat.

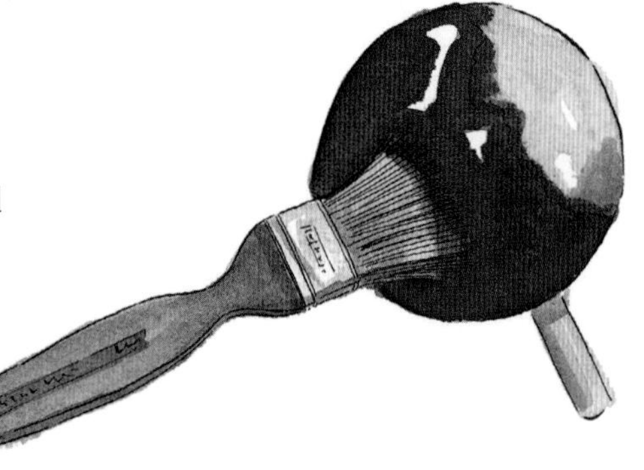

6 When the primer has completely dried, apply the adhesive for the gold leaf (follow the manufacturer's instructions).

7 Place the gold leaf over the tacky surface of the balls. Smooth over the backing surface before carefully peeling it off, leaving a layer of gold. Continue to apply the gold leaf, overlapping subsequent sheets, until the entire surface of each ball is covered. Rub off excess gold leaf but don't worry if the surface is uneven—this adds to the antique effect.

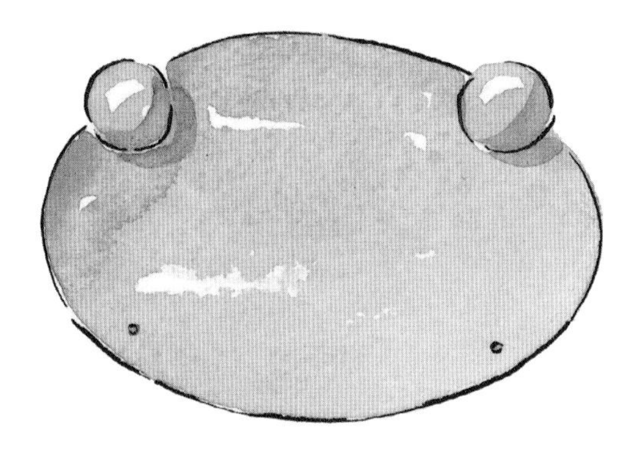

8 Drill four 3/8 in (7 mm) diameter holes into the plywood base to fit the dowels, positioning two at each end of the oval shape, close to the edge. Glue the dowels into the holes, pushing them in until the ball is touching the plywood base.

9 Insert the wooden base into the recessed stand of the washtub. Drill a few small holes through the base of the tub and the plywood stand to ensure good drainage.

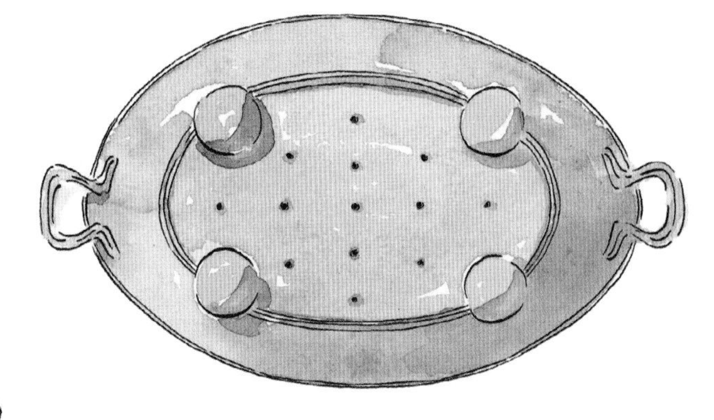

10 If your tub is a suitable color, you may wish to leave it unpainted. However, both enamel and tin can be painted to suit a particular planting plan. Gilding looks best against dark colors; navy-blue latex has been used here.

11 Fill the tub with moistened potting soil to 5 in (130 mm) below the top, forming a slightly dome-shaped surface. Remove the tobacco plants from their pots and arrange them in the tub; for a colorful and dense mound of flowers, mix the reds and pinks and position the root balls close together. Fill in the gaps with the remaining soil, firm in, and keep well watered. Place the moss around the plants to help retain moisture and for neatness.

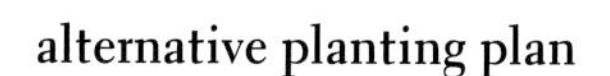

alternative planting plan

Place the tub indoors, in a kitchen or conservatory, or raise it on a low platform and plant with trailing ivy (*Hedera helix*).

wood

Wood provides the most varied selection of containers, from a formal 17th-century Versailles case to metal-banded coopered tubs. A wooden surface should be painted or stained—unless it is oak, which will weather to a pleasant silver-gray.

left This twig-work container planted with soleirolia is a variant on 19th-century rustic work. The sculpted character of this planter means that simple shapes and colors work best, allowing the design to be fully appreciated.

below left and far left A box standard and a chrysanthemum trained as a standard (far left) both make well-defined formal plantings for a Versailles case. Place cases in pairs flanking a front door or the entrance to a formal terrace or garden.

below The clump-forming perennial *Sedum spectabile*, shown here in a shallow wooden box, is a very useful container plant; its mass of foliage is as attractive as its compact, yellow-centered flower heads.

opposite, above left Evergreen shrubs create a dark mound that suits this tall coopered tub. Custom-made coopered planters have better proportions than halved barrels. If the steel bands are not galvanized, paint them to reduce rusting.

opposite, above center A paneled wooden window box has been planted with variegated ivy and *Capsicum annuum* 'Holiday Time.' Place at ground level on a paved terrace to act as a narrow border.

opposite, above right A Victorian shoe-cleaning box has found a new purpose as an eye-catching planter filled with chrysanthemums. If a box of this kind has not been painted or finished, treat it with wood preservative before planting.

opposite, below A shallow coopered tub has been planted with the poached egg plant (*Limnanthes douglasii*), which provides a useful mass of low white-yellow flowers to complement the water plants.

a rustic window box

The fashion for making objects covered in barked wood started in the 18th century. This design is based on the style of the English Regency landscape gardener Humphry Repton, who imitated the forms of classical architecture using rustic materials such as barked columns and pine-cone festoons.

MATERIALS & EQUIPMENT

exterior-grade plywood and surfaced softwood (see steps 1 & 2, page 70)
1 quart (1 liter) each clear wood preservative and green wood stain
14 ft (4.3 m) halved barked poles with 2–2½ in (50–65 mm) diameter
3 large and 8 small pine cones
no. 8 screws 1½ in (20 mm)
galvanized clout nails 3 in (80 mm)
finishing nails 2 and 2½ in (50 and 65 mm)
pot shards
30 quarts (30 liters) peat-based compost
3 male ferns (*Dryopteris filix-mas*)
6 crested female ferns (*Athyrium filix-femina cristatum*)
9 white cup flowers (*Nierembergia*)
small bag of sphagnum moss

1 Cut the following in exterior-grade plywood:
- 2 pieces for front and back ¾ x 10 x 36 in (18 x 250 x 900 mm)
- 2 pieces for sides ¾ x 6½ x 10 x in (18 x 160 x 250 mm)
- 1 piece for base ¾ x 8 x 36 in (18 x 200 x 900 mm)

2 Cut the following in surfaced softwood:
- 4 side supports 1 x 1 x 10 in (25 x 25 x 250 mm)
- 2 base supports 1 x 1 x 32½ in (25 x 25 x 810 mm)

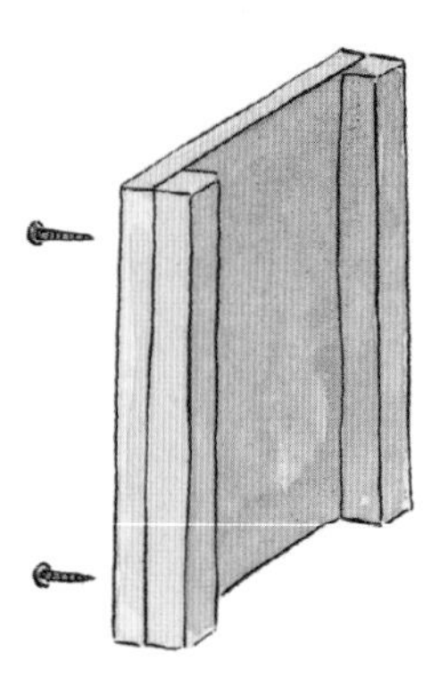

3 Drill holes for screws in each corner of the side pieces and screw the side supports flush with the long edges.

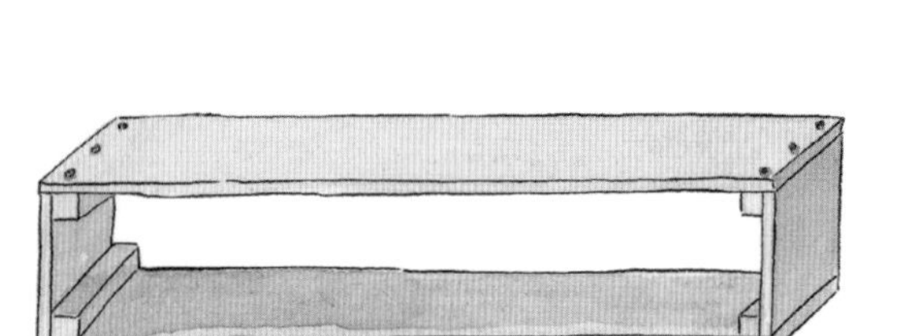

4 Drill holes along the short sides of the front and back pieces and place them flush with the outside edges of the side pieces. Screw into position.

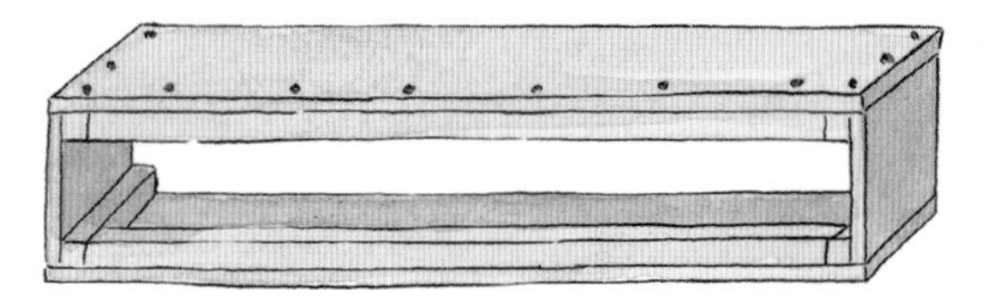

5 Slide the base supports between the side supports, flush with the base, and screw them in place through pre-drilled holes, front and back.

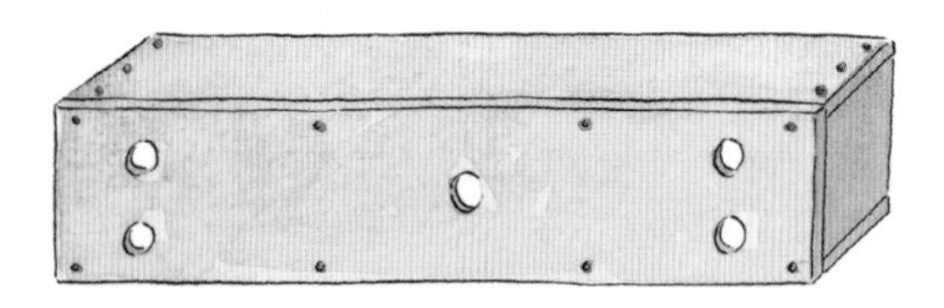

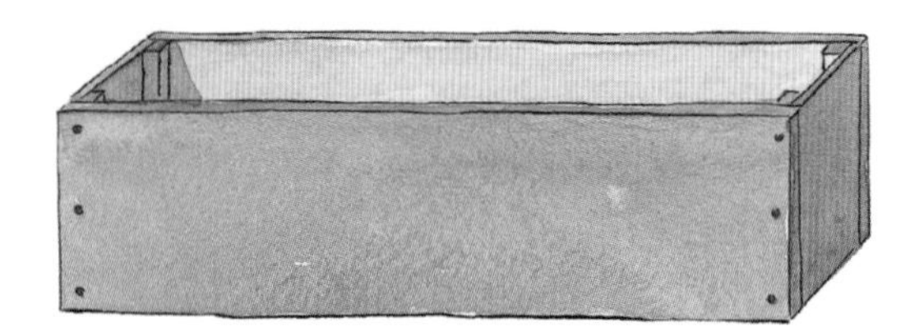

6 Use a power drill with a 1 in (25 mm) spade bit to drill five drainage holes in the bottom of the box, then screw it to the rest of the structure, driving the screws into the base supports.

7 Treat the box inside and out with wood preservative. When it has completely dried, apply the green wood stain to the front, back and sides, on the outside only.

8 To decorate the front of the box, cut four sections of halved barked pole, two 36 in (900 mm) long and two 10½ in (268 mm). Miter the ends of all four pieces, and use the 2½ in (65 mm) finishing nails to attach them to the front face; drive the nails in at an angle and make sure all the corners meet.

9 For the sides, cut six sections of bark-covered pole, each 10½ in (268 mm) long. Using three for each side, position the poles vertically and nail them into place.

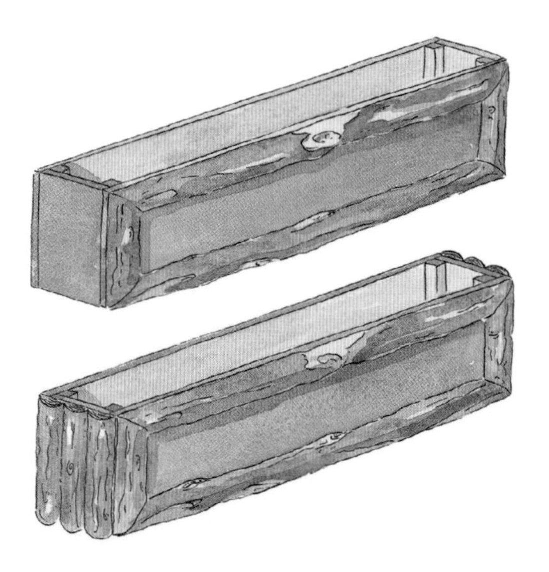

10 Cut one of the large pine cones in half lengthways with a hacksaw; use a vise to do this, or nail one half of the cone to a board, which will hold the cone steady while you cut. With the tip facing down, nail the half-cone to the center of the box with 2 in (50 mm) nails.

11 To complete the festoon effect, cut the small cones in half lengthwise. Use a vise or make a special cutting stand by gluing and nailing two pieces of 1 x 2 in (25 x 50 mm) lumber to a plywood board, placing them to fit the shape of the cone but leaving a gap at the top to allow for the saw. Push each cone between these rods and secure with nails, then cut in half with a hacksaw.

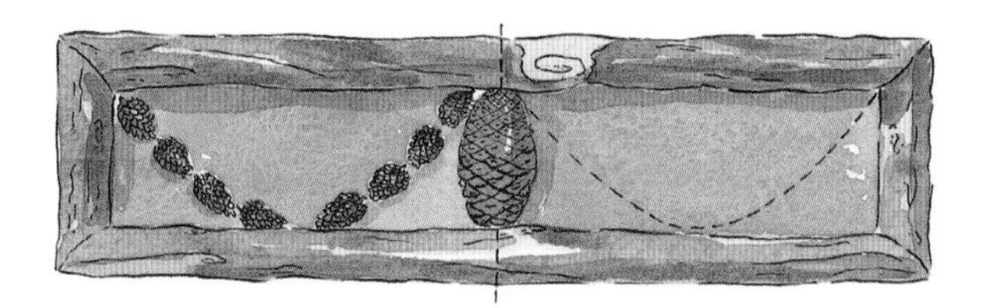

12 Draw two semicircles on each half of the front of the box. Glue and nail eight half-cones to each semicircle; start at the top and place matching pairs opposite one another with the tips facing down—if your cones are different sizes, put the largest ones at the top, graduating to the smallest at the central base of the festoon.

13 To construct the pine-cone finials, drill holes in the bottom of the two remaining large cones; make the holes big enough to accept half the length of the finishing nails. Insert the nails and then cut off the heads with a hacksaw.

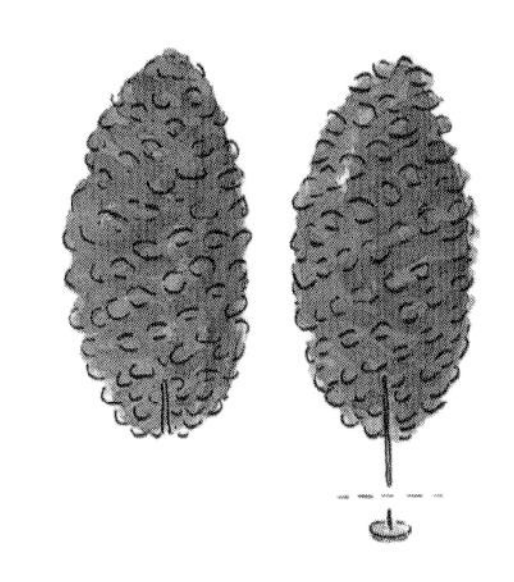

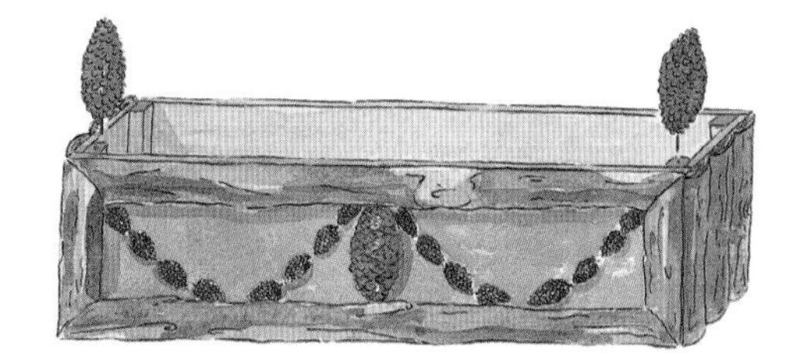

14 The finials are placed in the two side supports at the front of the box. Drill a hole for each and insert; secure them with a dab of waterproof carpenter's glue.

15 Line the base of the box with pot shards and half fill it with potting soil. Remove the plants from their pots and arrange as shown below, with the larger male ferns at the back. Add moistened potting soil to 1 in (25 mm) below the rim, pack down, and fill any gaps with moss. Water thoroughly. Consider carefully where to put the box; ferns need shade and regular watering although the moss will help retain moisture. White busy lizzies (*Impatiens*) can be used instead of cup flowers.

a Versailles case

A Versailles case is a wooden box that was used at the Palace of Versailles, in France, in the 17th century for growing exotics such as oranges, lemons, and palms, which could then be easily moved into the orangery or the greenhouses during the winter. A Versailles case can be unscrewed when the plants need repotting, or used as a decorative exterior for housing plants in plastic boxes or pots.

MATERIALS & EQUIPMENT

rough-sawn lumber (see step 1, page 74)
4 finials, balls, or pyramids with 1/2 in (10 mm) diameter dowels
1 piece of exterior-grade plywood 1/2 x 13 1/4 x 13 1/4 in (10 x 375 x 375 mm)
no. 8 screws 2 in (50 mm) and 1 1/2 in (40 mm)
waterproof carpenter's glue
1 quart (1 liter) exterior-grade wood preservative
wood stain or exterior-grade latex paint
pot shards
50 quarts (50 liters) potting soil (approximately)
New Zealand tea tree (*Leptospermum scoparium*)

1 Cut the following in rough-sawn lumbers:
- 6 side boards $^3/_4$ x 5$^1/_2$ x 15 in [1 x 6] (25 x 150 x 380 mm)
- 6 side boards $^3/_4$ x 5$^1/_2$ x 16$^1/_2$ in [1 x 6] (25 x 150 x 430 mm)
- 4 side supports 1$^1/_2$ x 1$^1/_2$ x 19$^1/_2$ in [2 x 2] (50 x 50 x 525 mm)
- 4 base supports 1$^1/_2$ x 1$^1/_2$ x 12 in [2 x 2] (25 x 25 x 280 mm)

2 Drill pilot holes in each corner of the six shorter side boards about $^3/_4$ in (20 mm) from the edge. The holes should be made to fit the 2 in (50 mm) screws. Do the same with the six longer side boards.

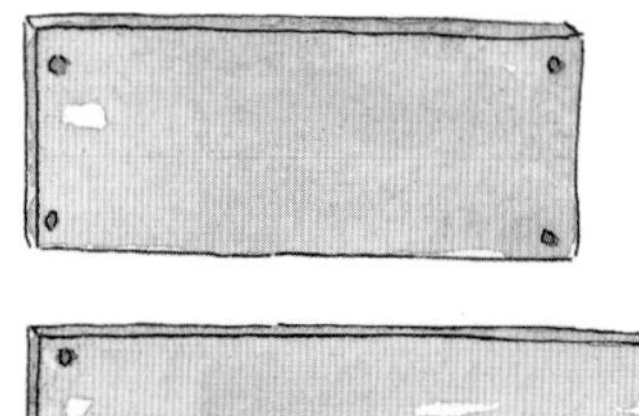

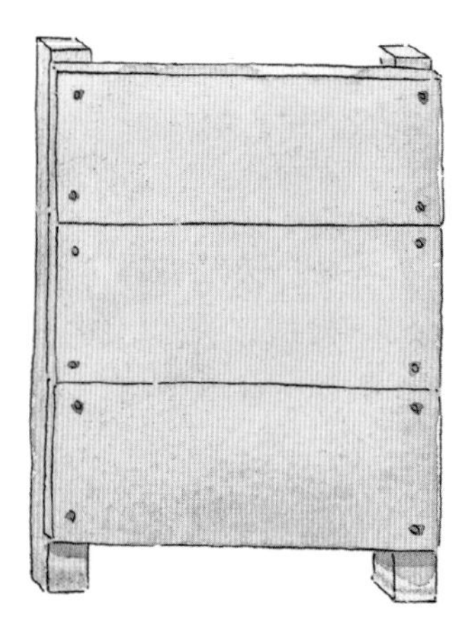

3 Using 2 in (50 mm) screws, attach the shorter boards to the side supports, flush to the edge, with a 2 in (50 mm) projection at the bottom and a 1 in (25 mm) projection at the top.

4 Using 2 in (50 mm) screws, attach the longer boards to the outside face of each of the side supports, creating a square-ended butt joint.

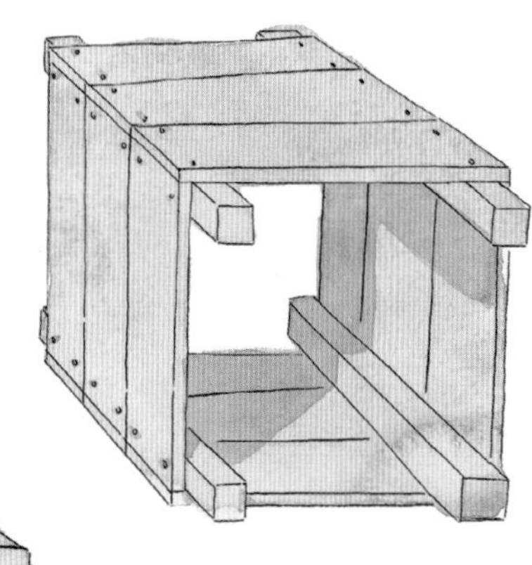

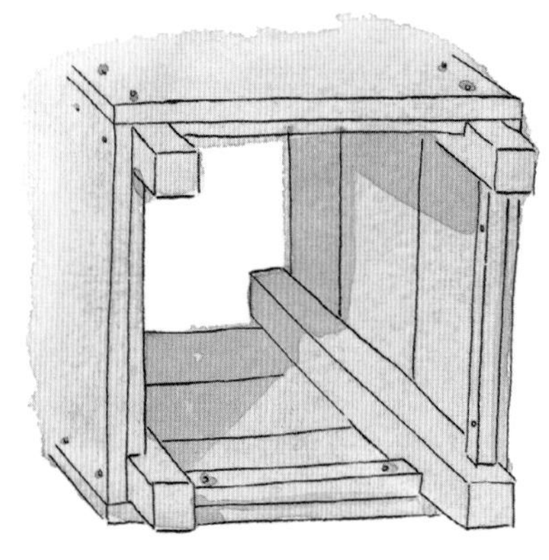

5 Prepare the base supports for 1$^1/_2$ in (40 mm) screws by drilling a hole about 1 in (25 mm) from each end. Place one support between each of the four side supports inside the box, positioning them at the base, flush with the bottom board. Screw into place.

6 To fit the base, cut a 1$^3/_4$ in (45 mm) square from each corner of the piece of plywood. Using a power drill with a 1 in (25 mm) spade bit, make five drainage holes, positioning them as shown. Drop the base into the case from the top; it should rest on the base supports secured in step 5.

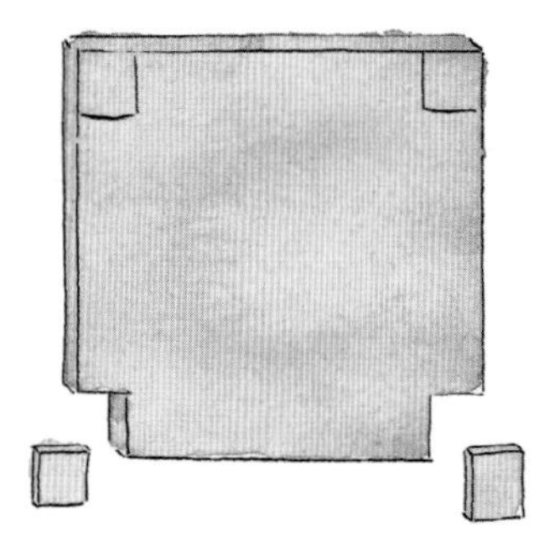

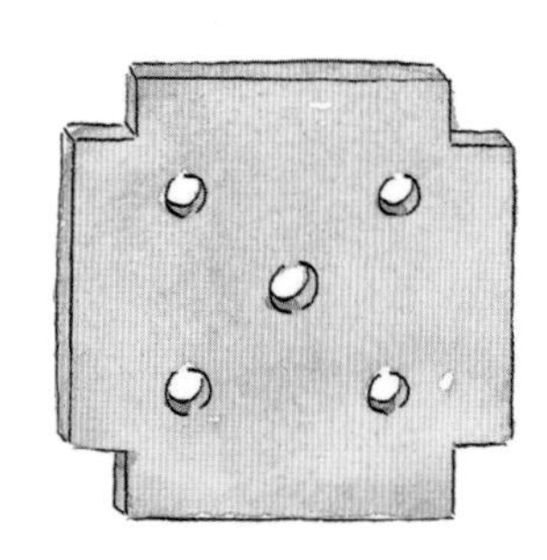

7 To attach the finials, drill in the top of each upright a ½ in (10 mm) diameter hole for the dowel, positioning it in the center. Use waterproof glue to secure the finial in the hole.

Alternatively make your own finials, putting them in place as shown on a separate 2 in (50 mm) dowel. Suitable designs for this size of case include a 2 in (50 mm) diameter wooden ball and a 5 in (130 mm) high pyramid cut from a 2 x 2 in (50 x 50 mm) rod. Place the pyramid atop a slightly smaller block.

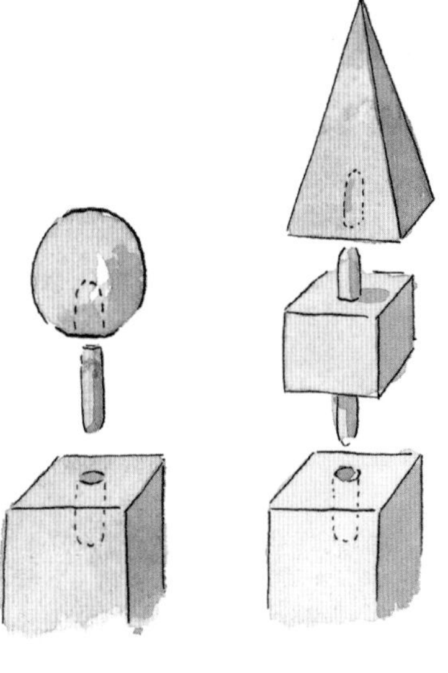

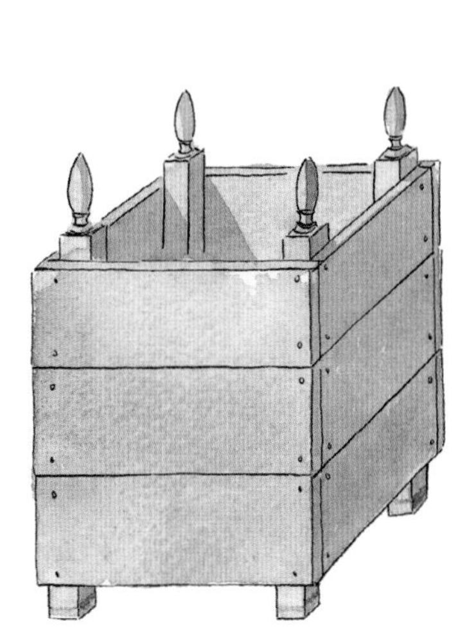

8 To protect the case, coat it in wood preservative inside and out. Then apply a wood stain or paint. Make sure the paint is thoroughly dry before planting.

9 Line the base of the case with pot shards. Take the plant from its pot and tease out the roots. Center the tree in the case and add moistened potting soil until the tree and surrounding soil are about 1½ in (40 mm) from the top of the case.

A flowering tea tree has been used here, but Versailles cases are also suitable for large shrubs, topiary, and masses of summer annuals.

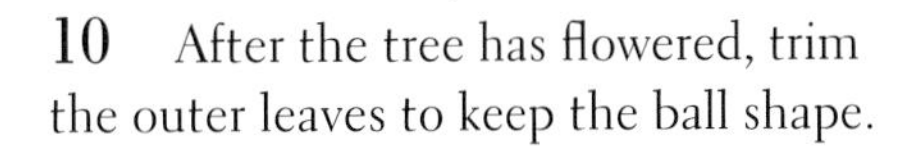

10 After the tree has flowered, trim the outer leaves to keep the ball shape.

a wood and trellis camouflage box

This container is designed to mask plants in plastic pots for seasonally changing arrangements. There is no base—simply fit it over your potted plants, enclosing the display within a decorated wooden case. A useful disguise for unattractive pots, the box also allows you to mix plant varieties that have different soil and feeding requirements.

MATERIALS & EQUIPMENT

2 pieces exterior-grade plywood 3/4 x 15 x 24 in (18 x 380 x 600 mm)

2 pieces exterior-grade plywood 3/4 x 15 x 22 1/2 in (18 x 380 x 560 mm)

4 pieces surfaced softwood 3/4 x 1 1/2 x 30 in [1 x 2] (50 x 50 x 750 mm)

44 ft (13.6 m) surfaced softwood for lattice 1/4 x 3/8 in (10 x 25 mm)

1 quart (1 liter) each exterior-grade wood preservative and exterior-grade latex paint

galvanized finishing nails 2 in (50 mm) and 1 in (25 mm)

waterproof carpenter's glue

no. 8 screws 2 in (50 mm)

16 standard sized bricks

4 marguerites (*Argyranthemum frutescens*) in 10 in (250 mm) plastic pots

1 To assemble the sides of the box, place the ends of the shorter boards against the inside face of the longer ones; glue in place, then reinforce with 2 in (50 mm) finishing nails. Mark a line 2 in (50 mm) from the top all the way around the box; the lattice will be fixed below this line.

To apply the lattice to the outside of the box, follow steps 2, 3, 4, and 5 for each of the four sides.

2 Measure and cut a length of lattice to form a diagonal strut. Lay it against the side of the box with its center line on the center line of the diagonal. Mark and miter the ends to match the corners of the box. Repeat for the other diagonal but cut a piece from the middle of the strut to fit. Glue and nail with 1 in (25 mm) finishing nails.

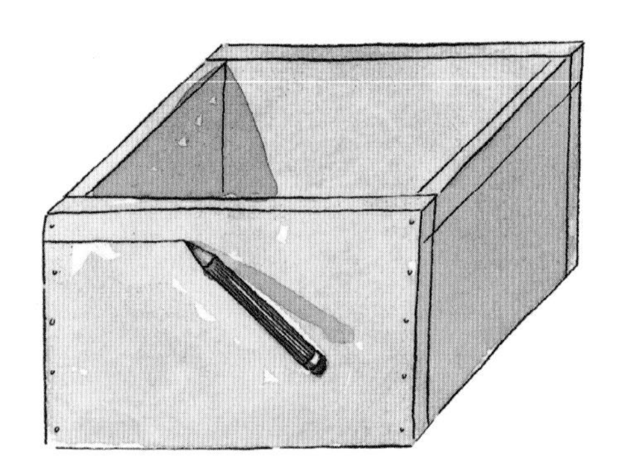

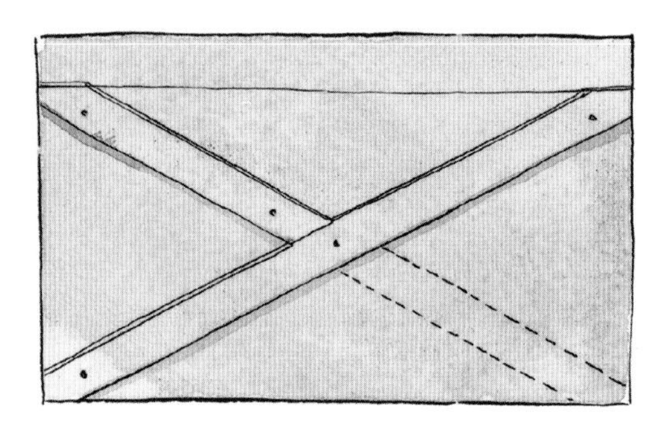

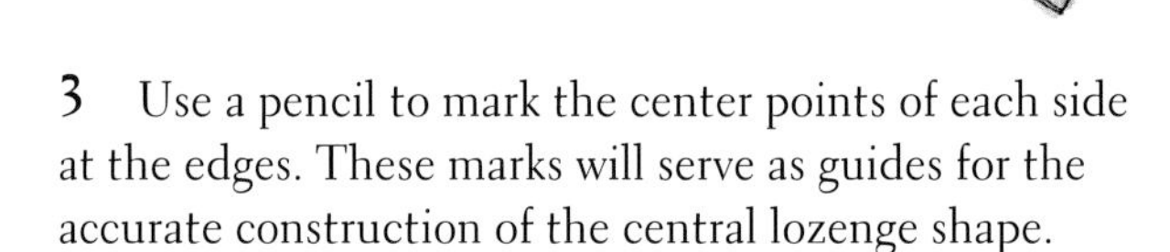

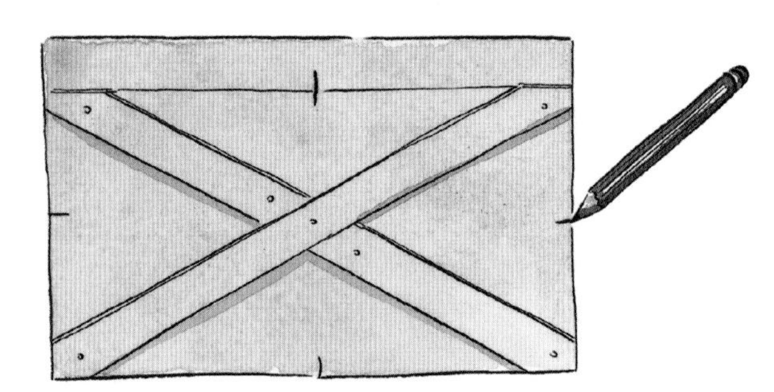

3 Use a pencil to mark the center points of each side at the edges. These marks will serve as guides for the accurate construction of the central lozenge shape.

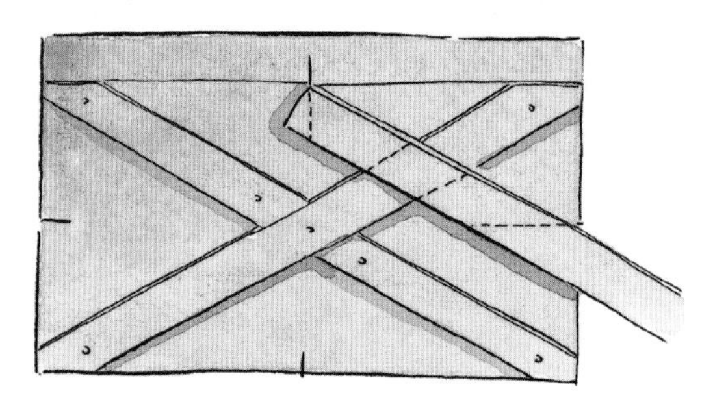

4 Make the first of the four diamond struts by placing a section of lattice in a line from a top or bottom center mark to a side mark. Cut a piece from the middle of this so it fits around the piece already in place and miter the ends.

5 Repeat step 4 for the other diagonals and fit them together on the box, matching the mitered ends. Glue and nail into place.

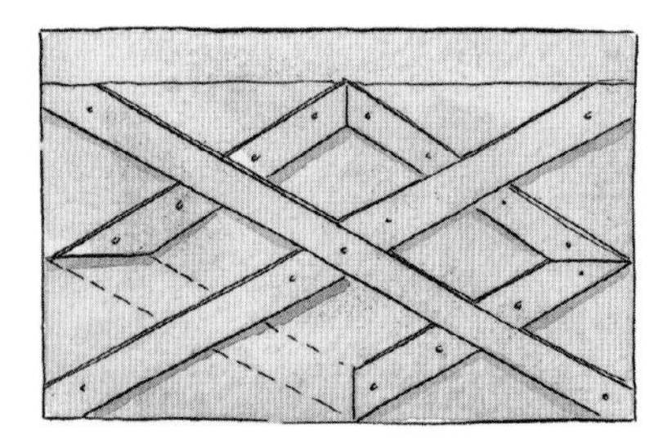

6 Treat all surfaces, inside and outside, with wood preservative and allow it to dry.

7 To form the top moulding, miter the ends of the four pieces of 1 x 2 so they fit together snugly around the top edge of the box.

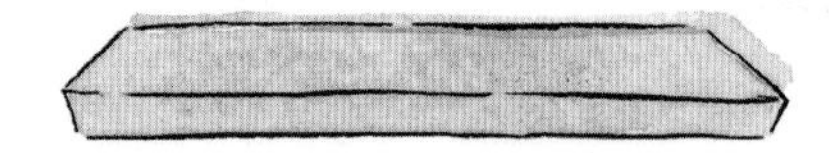

8 Drill screw holes along the top edges, then screw the molding to the box from the inside so it lies flush with the top edges. Reinforce the mitered corners with finishing nails. Coat the molding with wood preservative.

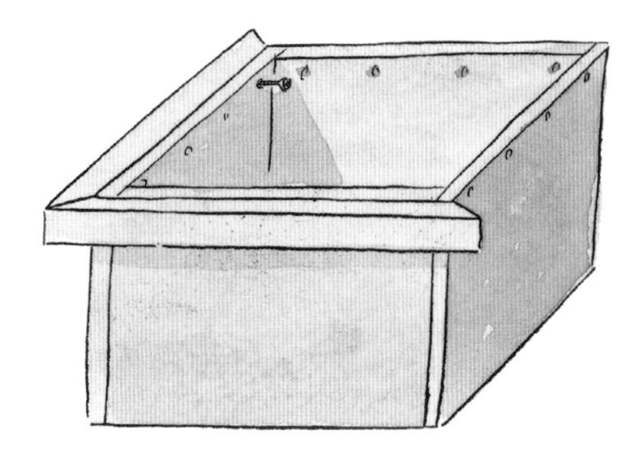

9 Apply two coats of paint in the color of your choice to the inside and outside of the box.

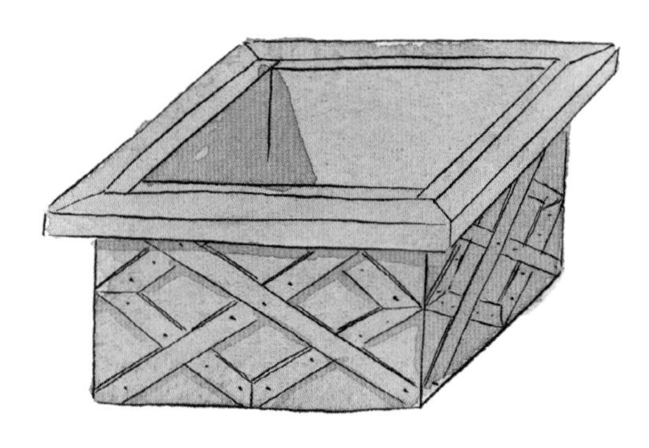

10 You may need to create a platform to make sure the tops of the pots rest just below the top of the molding. In this project four bricks have been placed under each of the pots so the pots sit ½ in (10 mm) below the top edge of the container; leave small gaps between the bricks to allow for drainage.

11 Place the plastic pots inside the container, one on each block of bricks. Marguerites have been chosen for this display because their mass of foliage and flowers works well with the proportions of the box.

alternative planting plans

4 *Fuchsia* x *speciosa* 'La Bianca,' 4 *Daphne odorata* 'Aureomarginata,' 4 common ivy (*Hedera helix* 'Erecta') around a common boxwood (*Buxus sempervirens*), 4 bear's breeches (*Acanthus mollis*), or 4 *Camellia japonica*.

a trough with trellis screen

This versatile trellis-backed trough is essentially a portable container for tall plants and climbers and can be moved around whenever you want to change your garden layout. It acts as both a screen and a planter and is ideal for use on a balcony or a rooftop garden where it may be difficult to support posts.

MATERIALS & EQUIPMENT

rough-saw lumber (see step 1, page 82)
no. 8 screws 1½ in (40 mm), 2½ in (65 mm), and 4 in (100 mm)
galvanized finishing nails 1 in (25 mm)
1 piece exterior-grade plywood ¾ x 13¾ x 33¾ in (20 x 345 x 845 mm)
45 ft (13.7 m) surfaced softwood ¾ in x 1¼ in [1 x 2] (20 x 30 mm)
1 quart (1 liter) wood preservative and about 2½ quarts (2½ liters) stain
pot shards
50 quarts (50 liters) potting soil (approximately)
1 *Trachelospermum jasminoides*
2 creeping myrtle (*Vinca minor*)
3 sky-blue creeping myrtle (*Vinca minor* 'Azurea Flore Plena')
10 *Petunia* 'Dark Blue Dwarf'

1 Cut the following pieces in rough-sawn lumber:

- 4 pieces for sides $\frac{3}{4}$ x $5\frac{1}{2}$ x 14 in [1 x 6] (25 x 150 x 350 mm)
- 4 pieces for front and back $\frac{3}{4}$ x $5\frac{1}{2}$ x 36 in [1 x 6] (25 x 150 x 900 mm)
- 4 uprights $1\frac{1}{2}$ x $1\frac{1}{2}$ x 12 in [2 x 2] (50 x 50 x 300 mm)
- 2 battens $1\frac{1}{2}$ x $1\frac{1}{2}$ x $31\frac{1}{2}$ in [2 x 2] (25 x 25 x 750 mm)
- 2 battens $1\frac{1}{2}$ x $1\frac{1}{2}$ x 11 in [2 x 2] (25 x 25 x 250 mm)
- 2 trellis supports $1\frac{1}{2}$ x $1\frac{1}{2}$ x 68 in [2 x 2] (50 x 50 x 1700 mm)

2 Drill holes for 2 in (50 mm) screws at both ends of the side boards. Use two boards for each side and screw them to the side supports, lining up the outer edges and staggering them so that two 2 in (50 mm) legs protrude from the bottom.

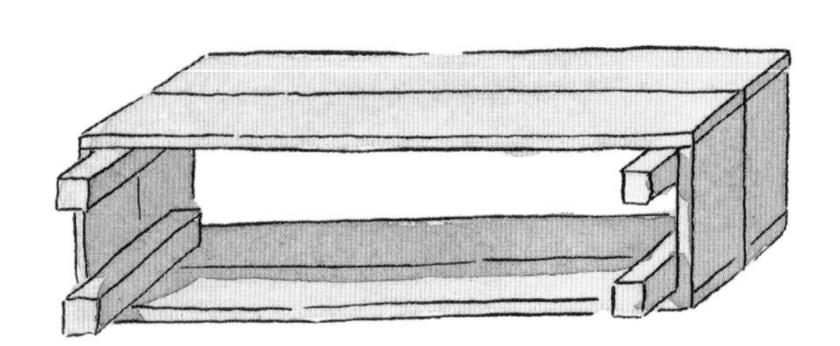

3 Assemble the box by screwing the front and back boards to the outside face of the sides; drill holes and use 2 in (50 mm) screws to secure the joint.

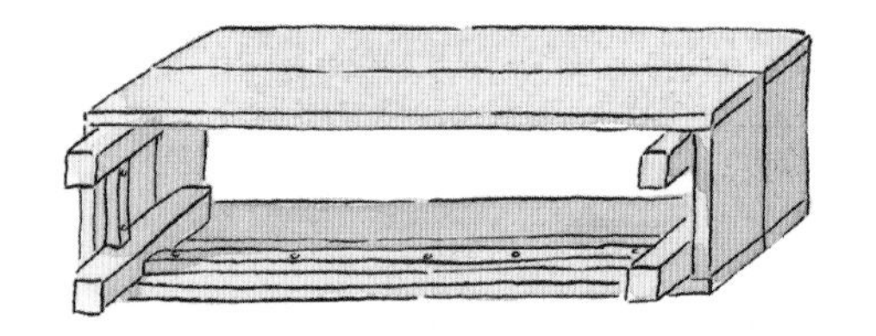

4 Drill the battens for the $1\frac{1}{2}$ in (40 mm) screws and place the battens between the uprights on the inside, flush with the base. Secure them in place with screws.

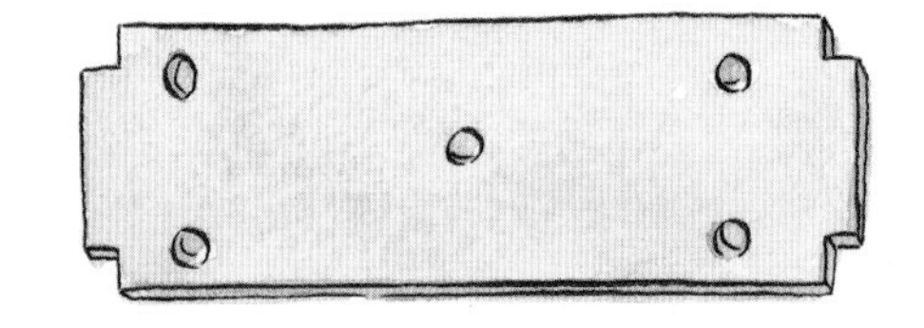

5 For the base, cut a $1\frac{3}{4}$ x $1\frac{3}{4}$ in (50 x 50 mm) square from each corner of the piece of plywood. Using a power drill with a 1 in (25 mm) spade bit, drill five drainage holes in the plywood. Slide the base into position atop the battens.

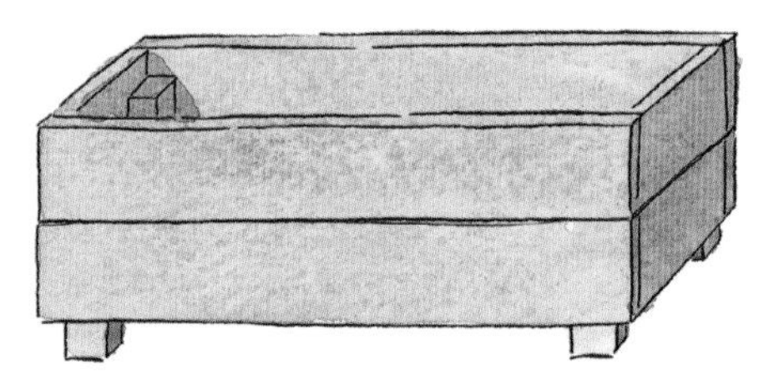

6 Treat the box and base with wood preservative. When it has dried, apply a couple of coats of stain.

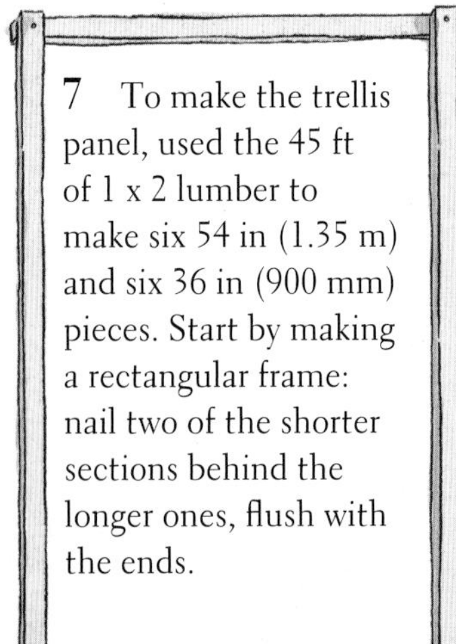

7 To make the trellis panel, used the 45 ft of 1 x 2 lumber to make six 54 in (1.35 m) and six 36 in (900 mm) pieces. Start by making a rectangular frame: nail two of the shorter sections behind the longer ones, flush with the ends.

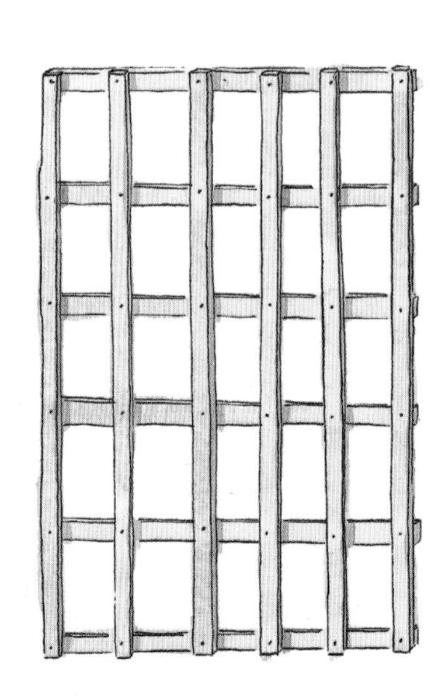

8 Divide each side into five equal parts and mark the divisions with a pencil. Nail the vertical sections of trellis first, top and bottom, and then the horizontals behind these, nailing at all junctions. Treat the structure and the trellis supports with preservative.

9 Drill the trellis supports for 2½ in (65 mm) screws and place them against the back of the trellis, flush with the top and sides. Screw in place from the front. Stain the trellis and supports.

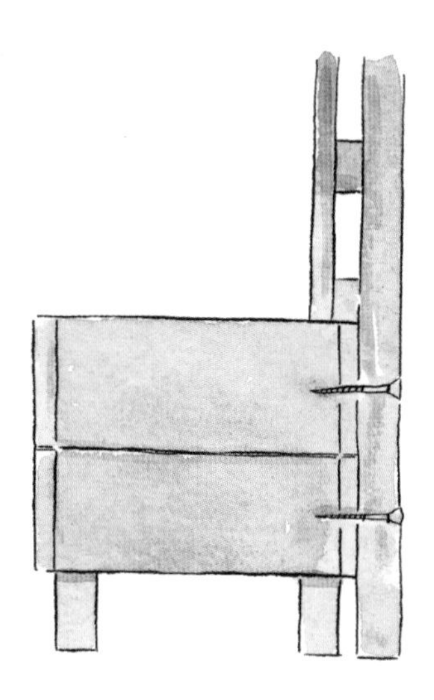

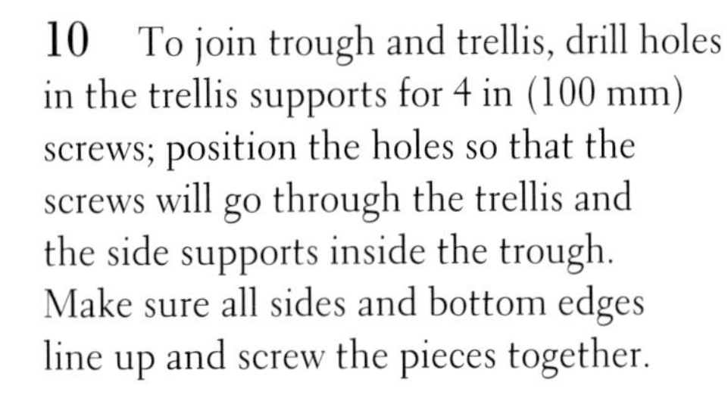

10 To join trough and trellis, drill holes in the trellis supports for 4 in (100 mm) screws; position the holes so that the screws will go through the trellis and the side supports inside the trough. Make sure all sides and bottom edges line up and screw the pieces together.

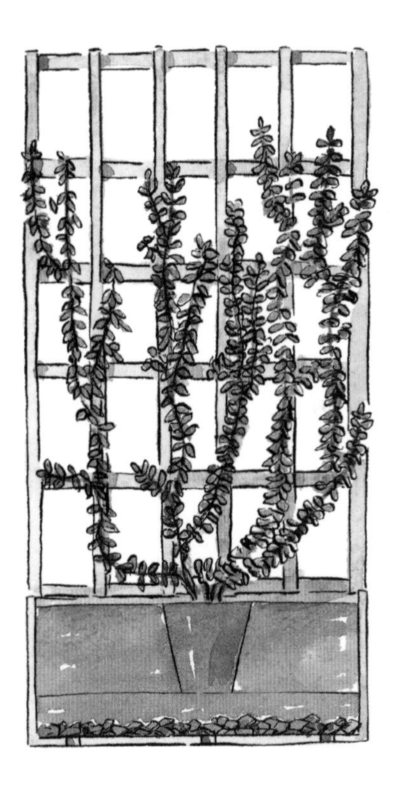

11 Line the trough with pot shards and enough moistened potting soil to ensure that the top of the plant sits about 1 in (25 mm) from the top edge. Use a tall trained jasmine for this project; if your plants are small, use two.

12 Place the plant in the center at the back of the trough, tease out the individual stems, and arrange them on the front of the trellis as evenly as possible; tie them to the trellis with coated wire.

13 Place the creeping myrtle along the length of the trough and fill in the spaces with dark blue petunias. Water thoroughly, and follow up with a liquid fertilizer every two weeks or so.

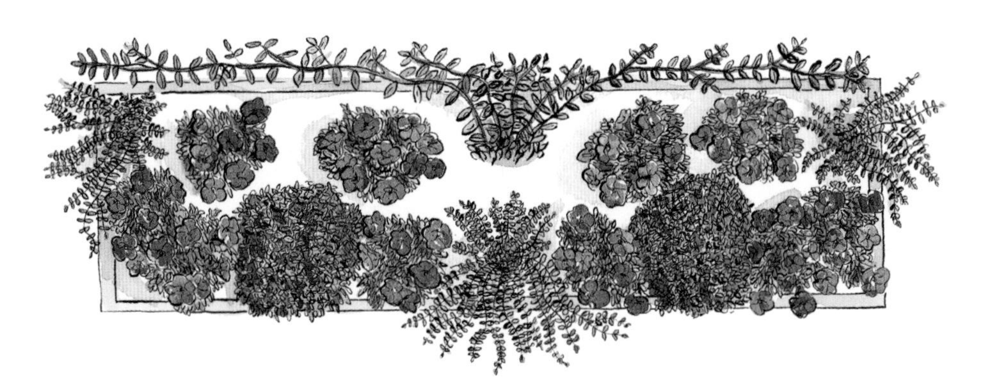

alternative planting plan

For a colder climate, plant the semi-evergreen wall shrub *Pyracantha coccinea*, underplanted with *Hedera helix*. For the trellis backing you could also use a more hedgelike plant such as a hawthorn or holly or even *Aucuba japonica*, which thrives even in very polluted environments.

planted gate piers

It is often useful to be able to raise plants up high so they can be appreciated from a distance. Use the planters in pairs to resemble gateposts or as part of a screen to mark a division in the garden. These wooden gate piers have been designed as cachepots—the individual plants remain in their plastic pots and can be changed seasonally.

MATERIALS & EQUIPMENT

1 piece exterior-grade plywood ½ x 48 x 96 in (12 x 1200 x 2400 mm)
2 pieces exterior-grade plywood ½ x 11½ x 11½ in (12 x 290 x 290 mm)
pressure-treated rough-sawn lumber (see steps 2, 3, 5, and 6 on pages 86–87)
2½ quarts (2½ liters) each exterior-grade wood preservative and exterior-grade latex paint
waterproof carpenter's glue
galvanized finishing nails 2 in (50 mm)
galvanized nails 1½ in (40 mm)
no. 8 screws 1¼ in (30 mm) and 3 in (75 mm)
4 *Hydrangea macrophylla*

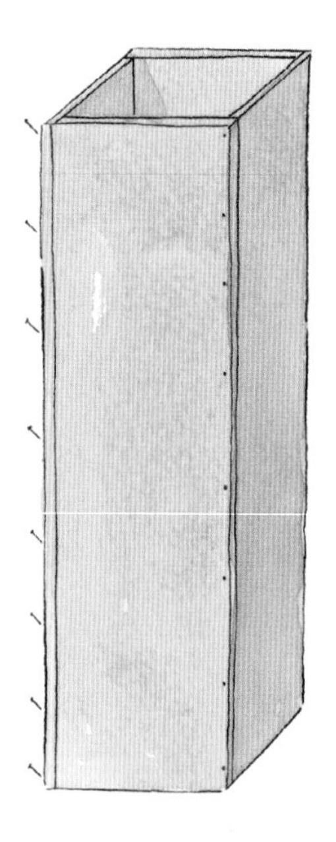

1 Cut the large piece of plywood into eight equal pieces, each measuring 12 x 48 in (300 x 1200 mm). Using butt joints, make two boxes by gluing the end of each board to the inside face of another; use finishing nails inserted at a slight angle.

2 For the base supports, cut four battens from the rough-sawn lumber, each 1 x 1 x 11½ in (25 x 25 x 290 mm). Position two battens on the inside of each box, opposite one another and 9 in (230 mm) down from the top. Drill holes in the plywood for 1¼ in (30 mm) screws. Glue the battens in place and secure with screws.

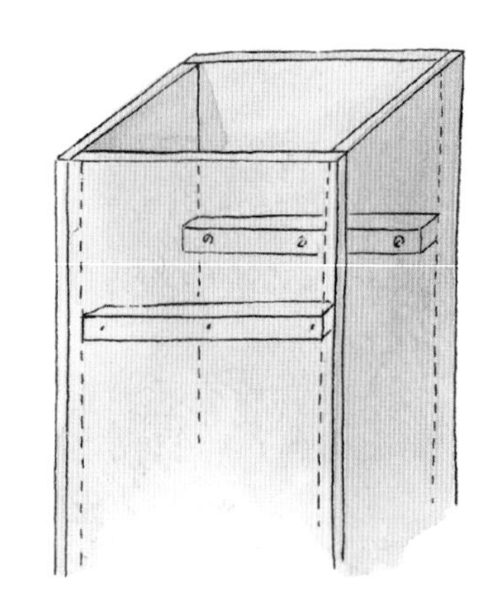

3 To make the top moldings, for each pier cut four pieces from the rough-sawn lumber each 2 x 2 x 16½ in (50 x 50 x 410 mm). Miter the corners. Glue and nail the moldings in place flush with the top edge and finish by reinforcing the mitered corners with finishing nails.

4 Treat the gate piers inside and out with wood preservative, making sure you coat the base thoroughly. When it has dried, apply two coats of paint to the outside and the inside down to the level of the base supports.

If the gate piers are to be placed on soil, follow step 5. To attach them to concrete or paving, follow step 6.

5 Make eight supporting stakes from rough-sawn lumber, each measuring 1½ x 1½ x 18 in (40 x 40 x 450 mm); sharpen one end on each to form a point. For each pier, hammer four stakes into the soil, spacing them to fit into the inside corners; the internal dimensions of the pier are 11½ in (290 mm) square. Leave 6–8 in (150–200 mm) of stake above the soil. Lower each pier over the stakes to sit on the ground and use a level to check that the pier is verticall. If the surface is uneven, bank it up with soil so the tops of both piers are level. Drill holes for 1¼ in (30 mm) screws in the bottom corners of the pier and screw the stakes to the plywood structure.

6 To attach the piers to concrete, cut four battens from rough-sawn lumber, each measuring 2 x 2 x 11½ in (50 x 50 x 290 mm). Using two for each pier, place them opposite one another with the outside edges 11½ in (290 mm) apart. Using masonry or concrete fasteners and the appropriate drill bit, fasten the battens to the surface. Slot the pier over the battens. Check they are level. Drill holes for 1¼ in (30 mm) screws and screw the piers to the battens through the sides.

7 Make the two plant shelves from the remaining squares of plywood. Using a power drill with a 1 in (25 mm) spade bit, drill five drainage holes. Treat both squares with wood preservative before dropping them onto the supporting battens inside each pier.

8 The gate piers are now ready to be planted by placing the potted plants directly onto the plant shelves. Hydrangeas have been used for this project, but the height of the base and pier can be adjusted to suit plants of different sizes and shapes.

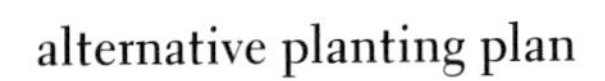

alternative planting plan

Other plants that would be suitable for this arrangement include a ball of boxwood (*Buxus sempervirens*) or marguerites (*Argyranthemum frutescens*). Keep all plants fed and watered according to their individual needs.

a wooden obelisk

Trellis obelisks have long been used as a decorative element in the garden. They create an attractive feature on their own, or in pairs frame a view or emphasize a formal approach to a house. The shape of the obelisk makes it suitable for supporting climbers such as ivy, clematis, honeysuckle, or hops. In this project, quick-growing hawthorn has been used; as the hawthorn spreads, use the trellis as a clipping guide to create a tall, elegant pyramid shape.

MATERIALS & EQUIPMENT

rough-sawn lumber (see steps 1, 2, 5, 6, and 13, pages 90–91)
square of exterior-grade plywood ½ x 15 x 15 in (12 x 380 x 380 mm)
no. 8 screws 1½ in (40 mm) and 2 in (50 mm)
galvanized finishing nails 1½ in (40 mm)
1 quart (1 liter) exterior-grade wood preservative
1 quart (1 liter) wood stain
50 quarts (50 liters) potting soil
pot shards
4 hawthorns (*Crataegeus monogyna*)

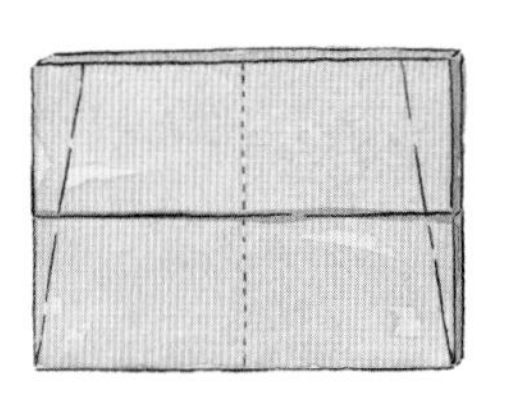

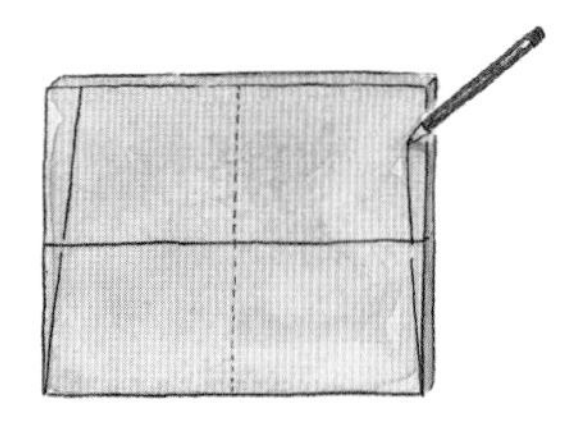

1 *For the short sides:* Use two boards ¾ x 5½ x 15 in [1 x 6] (20 x 150 x 390 mm). Lay the boards side by side and draw two lines at the angle shown above. Cut along the lines. Repeat with two more boards, so you have four angled short sides (two of each size).
For the long sides: Use two more boards ¾ x 5½ x 17 in [1 x 6] (20 x 150 x 430 mm). Lay the boards side by side and draw two lines at the angle shown above.
Cut along the lines. Repeat so you have four angled long sides (two of each size).

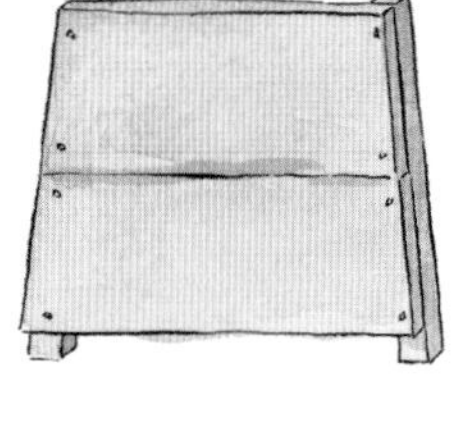

2 Take the two shorter sides and drill holes for 1½ in (40 mm) screws ½ in (10 mm) in from the tapered edges. Cut four corner supports from rough-sawn lumber 1½ x 1½ x 12 in [2 x 2] (25 x 25 x 330 mm), and position flush with the pre-drilled sides and top, leaving a 1 in (25 mm) projection at the bottom. Screw into place.

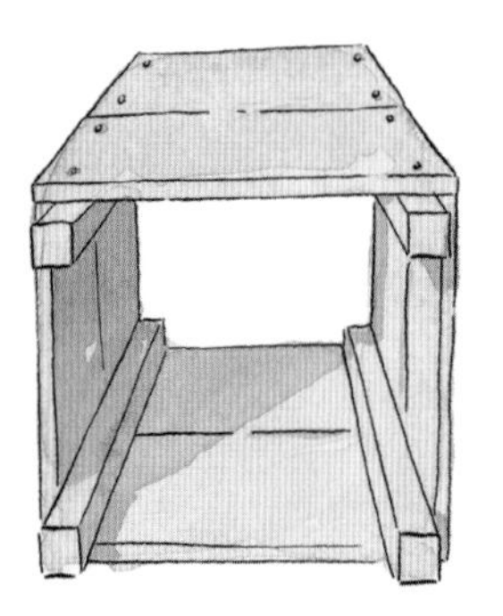

3 Position the longer sides against the outside face of the shorter ones, for a butt joint. Screw in place, making the holes 1 in (25 mm) in from the sides of the longer pieces.

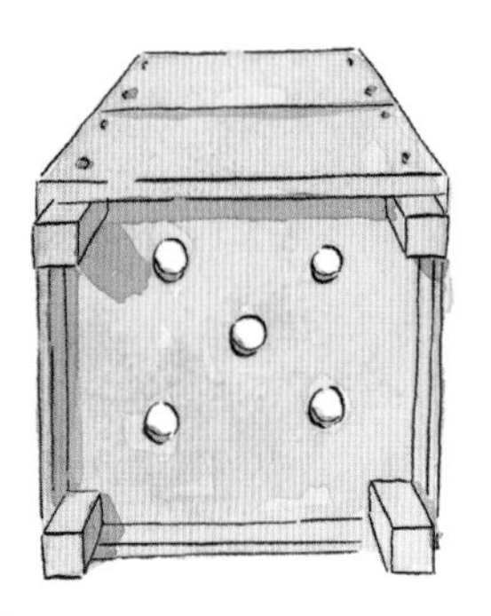

4 For the base, take the piece of plywood and cut a 1½ x 1½ in (40 x 40 mm) square from each corner. Drill five 1 in (25 mm) diameter drainage holes, as shown. Insert the base in position from the bottom of the tub before attaching the four base supports.

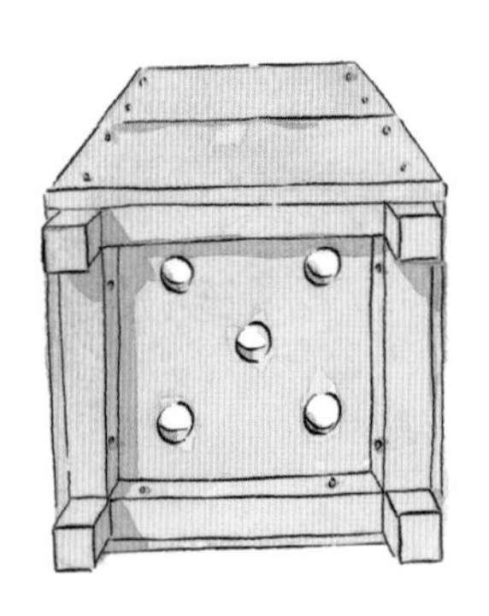

5 Cut four base supports from rough-sawn lumber 1½ x 1½ x 12½ in [2 x 2] (25 x 25 x 310 mm) and position flush with the bottom edge of the container on all four sides. Secure with 1½ in (40 mm) screws in pre-drilled holes.

6 For the obelisk, cut the following pieces:

- 4 side supports 1½ x 1½ x 90 in [2 x 2] (40 x 40 x 2350 mm)
- 60 ft (18 m) of lumber 1½ x 1½ [2 x 2] (40 x 40 mm), cut into lengths for rungs
- 1 block 4 x 4 x 4 in (100 x 100 x 100 mm) to form tapered top
- 1 board 1 x 4 x 4 in (25 x 100 x 100 mm) to form base of top

7 Place two side supports 4 in (100 mm) apart at the top and 19 in (480 mm) apart at the bottom. Cut and position one rung 5 in (130 mm) from the top and one 5 in (150 mm) from the bottom—make the rungs slightly longer than the actual width. Nail in place. Mark the positions of 14 rungs between them at 5½ in (140 mm) intervals. Repeat for the opposite side.

8 Cut and nail 14 rungs to the marked positions then cut off all overhangs flush with the side supports.

9 To assemble the obelisk, lay the two completed sections on their sides and cut and nail a top and bottom rung in place across them, positioning as in step 7. Mark the positions of the rest of the rungs as before then cut and nail them, making sure they line up on all sides. Repeat for the fourth side and cut off the overhangs.

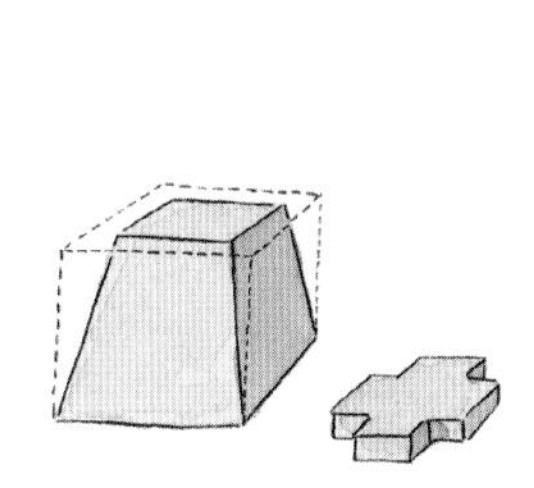

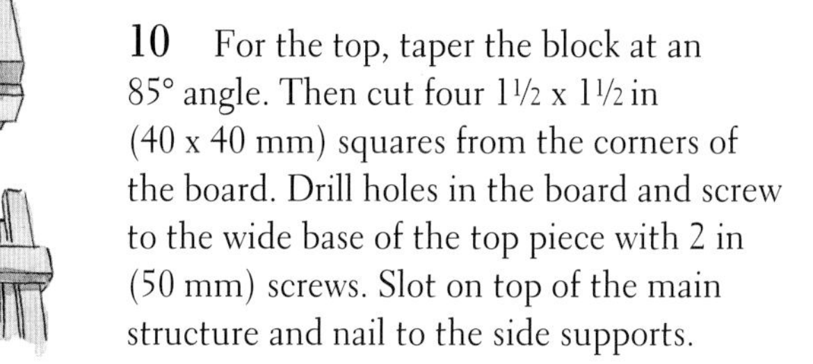

10 For the top, taper the block at an 85° angle. Then cut four 1½ x 1½ in (40 x 40 mm) squares from the corners of the board. Drill holes in the board and screw to the wide base of the top piece with 2 in (50 mm) screws. Slot on top of the main structure and nail to the side supports.

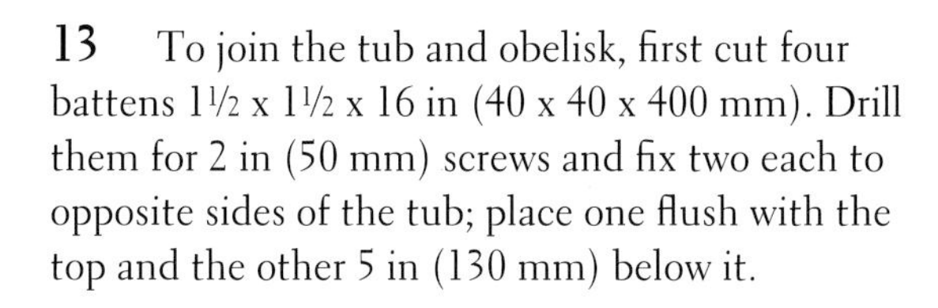

11 Before assembling the whole structure, treat the obelisk and tub with wood preservative. When the surface is dry, apply two coats of wood stain.

12 Line the bottom of the tub with pot shards. Fill the tub with soil and plant the hawthorns. The soil should come within 1 in (25 mm) of the tub's rim.

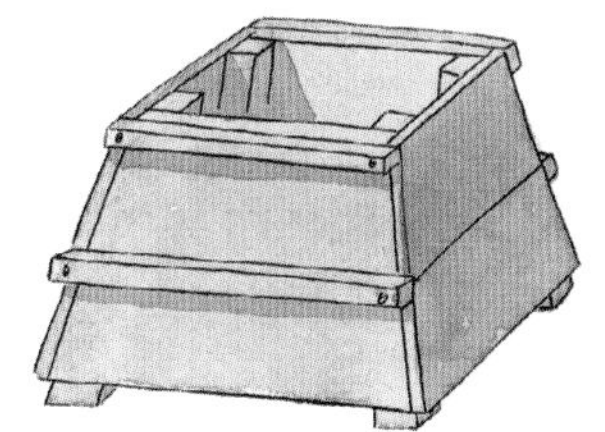

13 To join the tub and obelisk, first cut four battens 1½ x 1½ x 16 in (40 x 40 x 400 mm). Drill them for 2 in (50 mm) screws and fix two each to opposite sides of the tub; place one flush with the top and the other 5 in (130 mm) below it.

14 Fit the obelisk over the tub, making sure that the structure is square, and screw as above, attaching the bottom two rungs to the battens on the sides of the tub.

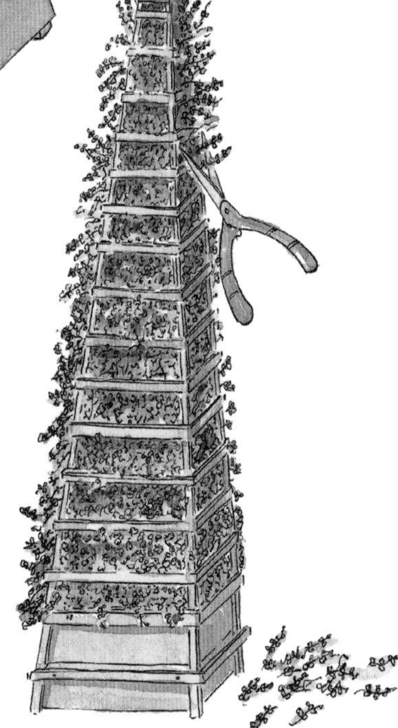

15 Make sure the tub is well watered and use a liquid fertilizer during the growing season. Use the trellis as a guide to clipping the hawthorn so that a tall slender green pyramid is achieved. Hawthorn may need clipping several times a year.

a primula theater

This design for a primula theater is for a scaled-down version of an early 19th-century type of shaded staging, made to show off the best examples in a collection and to protect the flowers from sun and rain. It will comfortably hold up to fifteen 4 in (100 mm) pots; terra-cotta pots look best. Paint or stain the theater dark blue, dark green, gray, or black to make a strong background for the rich and varied colors of the primulas.

MATERIALS & EQUIPMENT

surfaced softwood, rough-sawn lumber, and
exterior-grade plywood (see steps, pages 94–95)
1 quart (1 liter) wood preservative or oil-based primer
galvanized finishing nails
waterproof carpenter's glue
exterior-grade latex paint or wood stain
13 terra-cotta pots with 4 in (100 mm) diameters
Primula vulgaris
P. denticulata
P. veris
P. Gold Lace Group

Please note: This project is fairly complex. If you do not have good carpentry skills, you may want to consult a professional.

1 Cut the wood according to the diagrams and measurements.

front elevation

- 1 top piece ½ x 22 x 60 in (12 x 560 x 1520 mm) plywood
  A: 55 in (1395 mm)
  B: 21¼ in (540 mm)
  C: 8 in (200 mm) plywood
- 2 pieces 1 x 6 x 43¾ in (25 x 150 x 1110 mm) surfaced softwood
- 1 bottom piece 1 x 7 x 43 in (25 x 180 x 1095 mm) plywood

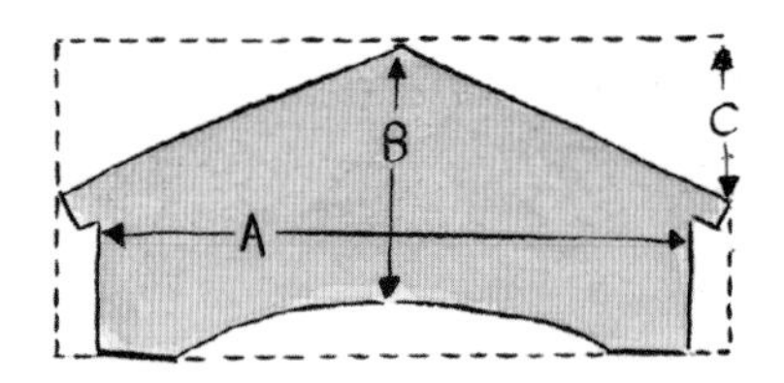

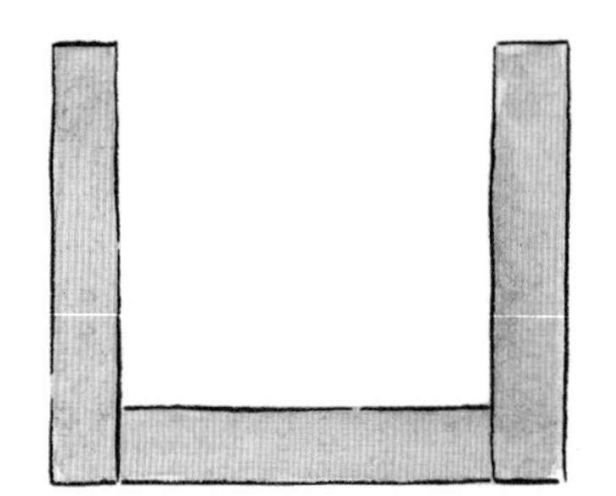

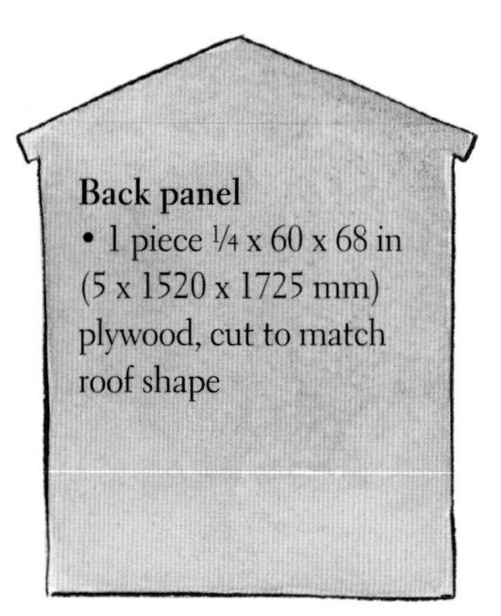

Back panel

- 1 piece ¼ x 60 x 68 in (5 x 1520 x 1725 mm) plywood, cut to match roof shape

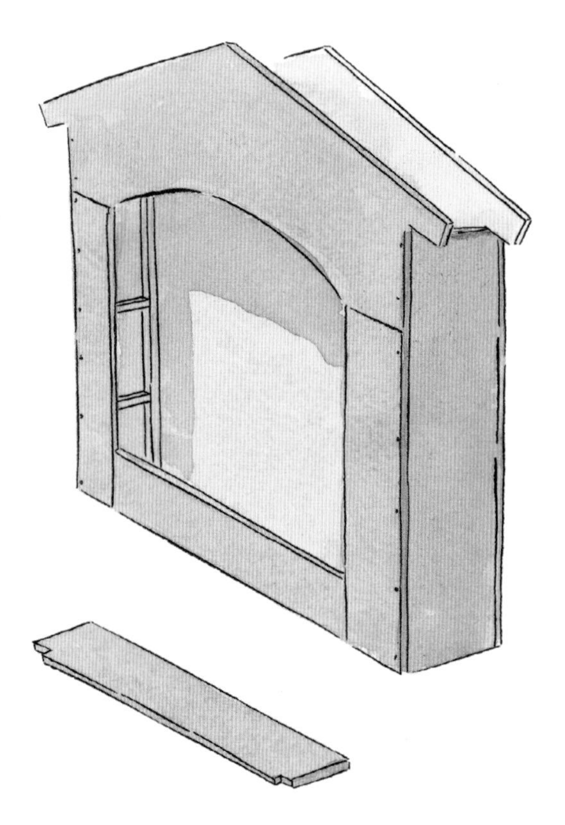

sides and supports

- 2 side panels ½ x 8 x 55 in (12 x 200 x 1395 mm) plywood
- 4 side supports 1 x 1 x 55 in (25 x 25 x 1395 mm) surfaced softwood
- 6 shelf supports 1 x 1 x 6 in (25 x 25 x 150 mm) surfaced softwood

2 To make up the sides, glue and nail the side supports to the outer edges of the two side panels. Then glue and nail the shelf supports 6, 19, and 31 in (150, 480, and 785 mm) from the bottom of the side panels. Glue and nail both completed sides to the plywood back.

3 Construct the frame by attaching the front elevation to the back and sides, gluing and nailing throughout.

4 Cut all the shelves but only attach the bottom one at this stage; sit it on the bottom side supports and glue and nail to the edge of the front elevation.

shelves

- 2 pieces 1 x 6 x 54 in (25 x 150 x 1370 mm) surfaced softwood
- 1 bottom piece 1 x 7 x 55 in (25 x 180 x 1395 mm) surfaced softwood with two two 1 x 1 in (25 x 25 mm) notches cut from both corners on one long side

5 Secure the roof supports as shown. Wipe off any excess glue. (The actual roof goes on last.)

roof supports

- 6 roof supports 2 x 2 x 8 in (50 x 50 x 200 mm) surfaced softwood

6 Cut out the upper and lower sections of the top pediment from softwood. Secure mitered edges with glue, reinforcing with nails. Glue and nail to the frame in the positions indicated—place the upper section first.

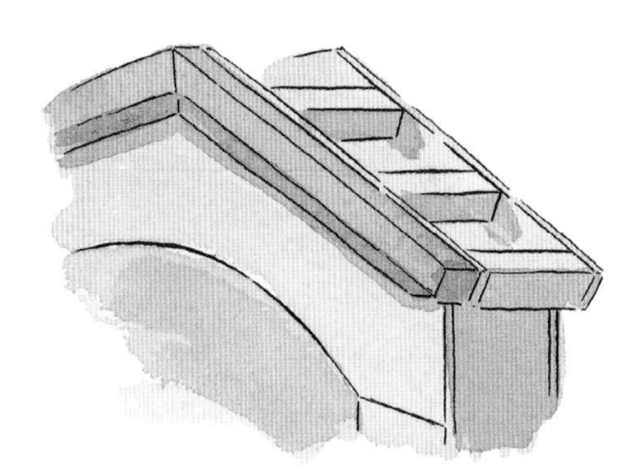

top pediment
- 2 upper sections 2 x 2 in (50 x 50 mm) approximately 30 in (760 mm) long to fit the size of the pediment, mitered at one end
- 2 lower sections 1 x 1 in (25 x 25 mm) approximately 30 in (760 mm) long to fit the size of the pediment, mitered at both ends

skirting
- 1 piece 1 x 7 x 57 in (25 x 180 x 1445 mm) mitered at both ends
- 2 pieces 1 x 7 x $10\frac{1}{4}$ in (25 x 180 x 260 mm) mitered at one end

7 Using softwood cut out the base pediment, the capitals, the base column, and the skirting, as highlighted in the diagram, from top to bottom. Secure in the same way as for the top pediment (see step 6).

base pediment
- 1 upper section 2 x 2 x 59 in (50 x 50 x 1495 mm) mitered at both ends
- 2 upper side sections 2 x 2 x $11\frac{1}{4}$ in (50 x 50 x 280 mm) mitered at one end
- 1 lower section 1 x 1 x 57 in (25 x 25 x 1445 mm) mitered at both ends
- 2 lower side sections 1 x 1 x $10\frac{1}{4}$ in (25 x 25 x 260 mm) mitered at one end

capitals
All pieces to be mitered at one end.
- 2 pieces 1 x 1 x $9\frac{3}{4}$ in (25 x 25 x 245 mm)
- 2 pieces 1 x 1 x 8 in (25 x 25 x 200 mm)

base column
All pieces to be mitered at one end.
- 2 pieces $\frac{1}{2}$ x 1 x $9\frac{3}{4}$ in (10 x 25 x 245 mm)
- 2 pieces $\frac{1}{2}$ x 1 x 7 in (10 x 25 x 180 mm)

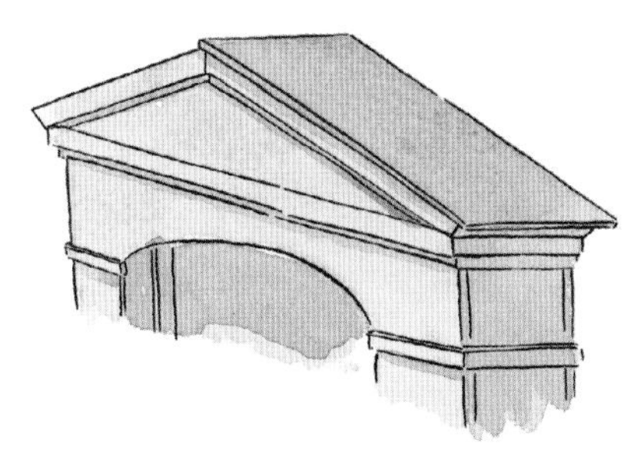

8 Cut out the roof pieces and nail in place, lining up the back edge with the back panel.

- 2 pieces $\frac{1}{2}$ x 12 x $30\frac{3}{4}$ in (10 x 305 x 780 mm) plywood, mitered at one end

9 Treat the theater and shelves with wood preservative. Finish by painting with an exterior-grade latex paint or stain. Make sure the shelves are totally dry and aired before placing plants, since preservatives and stains are often toxic to plants. Insert the two remaining shelves. Choose your plants from the selection listed. Plant them in shallow terra-cotta pots lined with pot shards and display on the shelves.

plant directory

Key

H = height S = spread Z = zones

Zone classifications are based on the average annual minimum temperature for each zone; the smaller number indicates the most northerly zone a plant can survive in; the higher number the most southerly zone the plant will tolerate.

Z1: below -50°F (-45°C)
Z2: -50 to -40°F (-45 to -40°C)
Z3: -40 to -30°F (-40 to -34°C)
Z4: -30 to -20°F (-34 to - 29°C)
Z5: -20 to -10°F (-29 to - 23°C)
Z6: -10 to 0°F (-23 to - 18°C)
Z7: 0 to 10°F (-18 to -12°C)
Z8: 10 to 20°F (-12 to -7°C)
Z9: 20 to 30°F (-7 to -1°C)
Z10: 30 to 40°F (-1 to 4°C)
Z11: above 40°F (4°C)

Acanthus mollis (Bear's breeches)
H: 3–4ft (90–120 cm); S: 4 ft (120 cm); Z: 8–10
Herbaceous perennial with large, beautifully shaped leaves, much used in classical ornamentation. White or pink flowers come in July to August on 18 in (45 cm) spikes. Prefers full sun.

Agapanthus africanus **'Headbourne Hybrids'**
H: 3 ft (1 m); S: 20 in (50 cm); Z: 7–10
Perennial that flowers in late summer. Deep blue-violet bell-shaped flowers and long evergreen leaves. Plant in well-drained soil in sun or light shade. Cover in winter or keep in a greenhouse.

Ageratum houstonianum 'Blue Danube'
H and S: 6 in (15 cm)
Summer-flowering annual with purple, blue, and pink heart-shaped flowers. Sow in a warm greenhouse and plant out late.

Anthemis nobile 'Treneague'
(Lawn chamomile)
H: 1 in (2.5 cm); S: 18 in (45 cm); Z: 4–8
Moss-like carpet of non-flowering grass with aromatic leaves; plant in a well-drained area.

Aptenia cordifolia 'Variegata'
H: 2 in (5 cm); S: indefinite; Z: 4–8
Low-growing perennial succulent. Cream-edged leaves and daisylike blue and pink flowers in summer. Prefers well-drained soil.

Artemesia 'Powys Castle'
H: 24–36 in (60–90 cm); S: 4 ft (1.2 m); Z: 6–9 Perennial dwarf, non-flowering, silver-leaved variety. Likes well-drained oil and full sun. Clip back in spring to keep compact.

Aster (Michaelmas daisy)
A genus of perennials and deciduous or evergreen shrubs with daisylike flowers. Prefers well-drained soil and a sunny aspect.

A. novae-belgii 'Audrey'
H and S: 12 in (30 cm); Z: 4–8
Pale blue, semi-double pointed flowers that open in fall.

A. novae-belgii 'Snowsprite'
H and S: 12 in (30 cm); Z: 4–8
Produces white slender-pointed flowers in fall. Plant in fall or spring.

Athyrium filix-femina cristatum
(Crested female fern)
H and S: 3 ft (90 cm); Z: 4–8
Fern with tall lacy fresh green crested fronds. Water freely March to October. Remove dead foliage in spring.

Buxus sempervirens

Calendula officinalis

Chrysanthemum frutescens

Aucuba japonica 'Crotonifolia'
H: 6–9 ft (1.8–2.7 m); Z: 7–9
Evergreen shrub that is best grown in shade. The speckled yellow and green leaves withstand urban pollution. 'Borealis' is a dwarf green variety.

Aurinia saxatalis
(syn. ***Alyssum saxatile***)
H: 9 in (23 cm); S: 12 in (30 cm);
Z: 3–7
Shrub with gray foliage and light yellow clusters of flowers. Likes full sun. Cut back after flowering.

Buxus sempervirens
(Common boxwood)
H: up to 15 ft (4.5 m); Z: 5–8
Medium-sized evergreen shrub or small tree that thrives in sun or shade. Most commonly used for dwarf hedges or for topiary. Produces luxurious masses of small dark evergreen leaves. Trim after growth in summer to maintain a uniform shape.

Calendula officinalis (Pot marigold)
H and S: 20–28 in (50–70 cm)
Annual with yellow to orange flowers in summer and fall. Likes well-drained soil and full sun. Self-seeds.

Camellia japonica
(Common camellia)
H: up to 30 ft (9 m); Z: 7–9
Evergreen lime-hating shrub or small tree with large flowers in varying colors in early spring. Will grow up to 6 ft (1.8 m) high in a large tub. Prefers acid to neutral peaty soil and will thrive in a lightly shaded position. 'Mathotiana Alba' is a good white double variety.

Campanula carpatica
(Bellflower)
H: 3–4 in (8–10 cm); S: 12 in (30 cm);
Z: 3–8
Rock perennial with blue, mauve, or lavender-blue flowers, either solitary or several to a stem. Flowers freely in summer in an open or semi-shaded position and well-drained soil.

Chaenomeles japonica 'Alba'
H: 3–12 ft (1–3.7 m); Z: 4–8
Deciduous shrub with white flowers in early spring. This plant will happily grow in a shaded environment. It is advisable to cut back the plant immediately after flowering in order to preserve its compact shape.

Chrysanthemum frutescens
(syn. ***Argyranthemum frutescens***)
(Marguerites)
H and S: 3 ft (1 m); Z: 8–10
Shrubby perennial with grayish foliage and white or yellow daisylike flowers with yellow centers. Flowers for a long period in summer if deadheaded. Train as a standard or tight ball by pinching out the foliage ends. Do not put out until end of May.

Citrus limon 'Meyer'
H: 18–24 in (45–60 cm);
S: 18–20 in (45–50 cm); Z: 9–10
Evergreen medium to large shrub with large bright green leaves and heavily scented white flowers in spring and summer followed by large lemons; flowers and fruits together. Overwinter in a greenhouse or conservatory; may be put outside after frosts in a sheltered sunny place. Keep well watered in summer.

Convolvulus sabatius
(syn. ***C. mauritanicus***)
H: 6–8 in (15–20 cm); S: 12 in (30 cm);
Z: 8–10
Rock trailing perennial with blue-mauve flowers.

Crataegus monogyna

Delphinium Belladonna 'Wendy'

Fuchsia x *speciosa* 'La Bianca'

Coreopsis tincturia (Tickseed)
H: 2–3 ft (60–90 cm); S: 8 in (20 cm)
Annual with yellow to crimson brown-edged flowers in summer. Colored hybrids also available.

Cordyline indivisa
(syn. ***Dracaena indivisa***)
H: 10 ft (3 m); S: 6 ft (2 m); Z: 8–10
Evergreen tree or shrub with long spiky leaves—gray with red or yellow stripe.

Crataegus monogyna
(Common hawthorn)
H: up to 20 ft (6 m); Z: 4–7
Quick-growing deciduous small tree. White flowers and red fruit and fall foliage. Clip throughout growing season.

Cyclamen
A genus of tuberous perennials with pendulous flowers and five reflexed petals. Likes a sunny aspect and well-drained soil.
C. cilicium
H: 4 in (10 cm); S: 2–4 in (5–10 cm); Z: 6–9
Roundish leaves with silvery markings and pale pink flowers in fall.
C. hederifolium
H: 4 in (10 cm); S: 2–4 in (5–10 cm); Z: 5–9
Ivy-shaped leaves with scented pink flowers in fall, from September to October.

Daphne odora 'Aureomarginata'
H and S: 5 ft (1.5 m); Z: 4–7
Dwarf evergreen spreading shrub. Narrow leaves have a yellow margin and the white flowers are very fragrant. Plant in a sunny sheltered position.

Delphinium Belladonna 'Wendy'
H: 24 in (60 cm); S: 8 in (20 cm); Z: 5–9
Perennial with gentian-blue flowers in summer. Also pale blue, white, and pink.

Dryopteris filix-mas (Male fern)
H and S: 16 in (40 cm); Z: 4–9
Deciduous or semi-evergreen bright green fern. Needs shade and humus-rich soil. Keep moist.

Exacum affine (Persian violet)
H: 6 in (15 cm)
Annual with bluish lilac fragrant flowers from June to October. Water freely and overwinter indoors.

Festuca glauca
(Blue fescue)
H and S: 23 cm (9 in); Z: 4–8
Perennial thin-leaved grass forms bright blue to gray dense tufts. At its best in the sun from spring to midsummer.

Fuchsia
Genus of deciduous shrubs with pendulous bell-shaped flowers. Plant in a sunny place and cover roots with mulch.
F. 'Margaret'
H: 3 ft (1 m); S: 2½ ft (75 cm); Z: 9–10
Vigorous shrub. Crimson and violet-purple semi-double flowers.
F.* x *speciosa 'La Bianca'
H and S: 2 ft (60 cm); Z: 9–10
Hybrid shrub with pink flowers. Overwinter in a cool greenhouse, put out in May. Train as a half or full standard.

Gazania 'Orange Beauty'
H and S: 12 in (30 cm); Z: 5–9
Perennial with silver-gray foliage; brilliant orange flowers appear from late June. Plant in late May in light sandy soil in sun. Protect from frost. A variety of colors is available.

Hebe pinguifolia 'Pagei'
H: 6–12 in (15–30 cm);
S: 2–3 ft (60–100 cm); Z: 7–9.
Dwarf evergreen gray-leaved shrub. Forms very satisfactory mounds of gray foliage. White flowers in late spring.

Helianthus 'Lodden Gold'

Heliotropium peruvianum 'Royal Marine'

Hydrangea macrophylla 'Blue Wave'

Hedera (Ivy)
A genus of evergreen woody-stemmed, trailing perennials with green or variegated lobed leaves. Prefers well-drained soil.
H. helix (Common English ivy)
H and S: up to 10 ft (3 m); Z: 6–9
Climbing or trailing evergreen, also "self-branching." Can be trained over frames. Varieties include *H. helix* 'Glacier,' *H. helix* 'Autropureum,' and *H. helix* 'Adam.'
***H. helix* 'Erecta'** (Upright ivy)
H: 30 ft (10 m); S: 15 ft (5 m); Z: 6–9
Useful clipped in window boxes as an alternative to boxwood or as a year-round support structure for seasonal planting.

***Helianthus* 'Loddon Gold'**
(Sunflower)
H: 4–5 ft (1.2–1.5 m)
Annual with double golden yellow flowers from July to September. Needs sun.

Heliotropium peruvianum
'Royal Marine' (Heliotrope, Cherry Pie)
H: 15–36 in (38–90 cm);
S: 12–15 in (30–38 cm); Z: 9–10
This purplish green-leaved perennial has heavily scented violet-blue flowers. Plant in a sunny position in early June. Overwinter in a conservatory or a cool greenhouse. Can be trained as a standard on a cane.

***Holcus mollis* 'Albovariegatus'**
(Creeping softgrass)
H: 12–18 in (30–45 cm); S: indefinite;
Z: 4–9
Evergreen, spreading perennial grass with white-and-green varigated foliage. In summer it carries purplish-white flower spikes.

Hosta
A genus of herbaceous perennials grown for abundant foliage ranging from blues to silver-green and golden colors. Will tolerate shade and prefers damp soil.
H. fortunei var. ***aureamarginata***
H: 2 ft (60 cm); Z: 3–9
Leaves are edged in yellow and late spring flowers are lilac.
H. sieboldiana var. ***elegans***
H: 2–3 ft (60–90 cm); Z: 3–9
Bold blue-green foliage and violet flowers in early summer.

***Hyacinthus orientalis* 'Delft Blue'**
H: 10 in (25 cm); S: 6 in (15 cm); Z: 4–8
Pale blue heavily scented flowers are produced from a bulb in April. Plant from mid-September. Water well when growing. Other colors and dwarf varieties are also available.

***Hydrangea macrophylla* 'Blue Wave'**
(Lace cap hydrangea)
H: up to 6 ft (1.8 m); Z: 6–9
Deciduous shrub. Dense heads of variable blue flowers in summer. In alkaline soils flowers change to pink. Add aluminum sulphate to change back to blue.

Ilex (Holly)
Evergreen deciduous trees or shrubs with glossy green foliage and berries. Tolerates sun and shade. Prefers well-drained soil.
***I.* x *meserveae* 'Blue Prince'**
H: up to 10 ft (3 m); Z: 7–9
Vigorous growth of dark blue-green foliage.
***I. aquifolium* 'Silver Queen'**
H: 20 ft (5 m); S: 12 ft (4 m); Z: 7–9
Variegated leaves of green mottled gray with white margins and reddish stems and no berries. Often grown as a standard. Clips well into dense formal shape. Is paradoxically a male plant.
I. crenata
H: 15 ft (5 m); S: 10 ft (3 m); Z: 6–8
Tiny boxwoodlike dark green leaves. Keeps a compact shape when pruned.

Impatiens balsamina (Busy lizzy)
H: 9 in (23 cm); Z: 5–9
Annuals available in many colors with both double and single flowers. Put in a sheltered sunny location in rich moist soil.

Leptospermum scoparium

Lilium 'Reinesse'

Myosotis alpestris

Laurentia axialaris 'Blue Star'
H: 6 in (15 cm)
Small-growing annual related to lobelia. Pale blue mauve flowers from June onward and light green foliage. Plant in full sun in well-drained soil.

Leptospermum scoparium (Tea tree)
H: up to 10 ft (3 m); Z: 9–10
Evergreen shrub with dark grayish green leaves and small pink long-lasting flowers that begin in early summer. Overwinter in a cool greenhouse. Good flowering topiary subject; clip to retain dense foliage head.

Lilium 'Reinesse'
H: 12 in (30 cm); Z: 4–9
Bulb produces pale yellow or white flowers in summer. Likes well-drained soil. Deadhead and keep out of direct sun.

Linaria cymbalaria (Ivy-leaved toadflax)
H: 4–6 in (10–15 cm); Z: 4–8
Trailing perennial with lilac flowers in summer. Good in hanging baskets. Water well in summer; keep almost dry in winter.

Lobelia erinus 'Pendula Blue Cascade'
H: 4–8 in (10–20 cm); S: 4–6 in (10–15 cm)
Trailing annual. Light blue flowers in summer. Good in hanging baskets.

Morus alba 'Pendula'
(Weeping mulberry)
H: 6–8 ft (1.8–2.5 m); Z: 4–10
Deciduous tree with attractive weeping foliage and mulberry fruit. Protect from strong winds. Prune in February, thinning overcrowded branches. Plant from October to March.

Myosotis alpestris (Forget-me-not)
H and S: 6–9 in (15–23 cm)
Biennial or perennial. Pot early fall. Pale blue flowers appear in mid-spring to early summer. A beautiful feathery underplanting for tulips. Available in white and various dark blues.

Nemesia caerulea
H: 10 in (25 cm)
Annual, plant out in June in sun. Propagate by seed sown in March.

Nicotiana (Tobacco plant)
Genus of perennials treated as annuals with tubular scented flowers. Plant in well-drained soil for summer flowering.
N. alata **'Lime Green'**
H: 2 ft (60 cm); S: 1 ft (30 cm)
Lime-green flower; sow seed in warm greenhouse February to March. Keep well watered. Available in dwarf forms.

N. **'Domino Pink'**
H and S: 18 in (30 cm)
Bushy plants characterized by bright magenta pink flowers. Other colors available in Domino Series.

Osteospermum
Genus of evergreen semi-woody perennials. Suits a sunny aspect and well-drained soil. Produces sprawling daisylike flowers in summer to early fall.
O. **'Buttermilk'**
H: 2 ft (60 cm); S: 1 ft (30 cm); Z: 6–9
Large butter-yellow daisylike flowers with dark eyes.
O. **'Whirly Gig'**
H: 2 ft (60 cm); S: 12–18 in (30–45 cm); Z: 6–9
White paddle-shaped petals.

Pelargonium 'Balcon Royale'
Trails: 12–24 in (30–60 cm)
Perennial grown as annual. Ivy-leaved pelargonium with bluish red flowers in mid-spring to mid-fall. Overwinter indoors and display in dry sunny conditions.

Pelargonium 'Friesdorf'
H: 10 in (25 cm); S: 6 in (15 cm)
Zonal evergreen perennial characterized by dark green foliage and scarlet-orange flowers with thin petals.

Nicotiana 'Domino Pink'

Osteospermum 'Whirly Gig'

Petunia

Petunia
A genus of annuals characterized by showy flowers in a variety of colors, either Grandiflora or Multiflora. They need plenty of sun and well-drained soil.
P. surfina
H: 9–12 in (23–30 cm)
Numerous named hybrids are also available. Plant out late May to June and deadhead to make the most of the long flowering season.
***P.* 'Dark Blue Dwarf'**
H: 8 in (20 cm)
Rich blue flowers; suited to small pots.
***P.* 'Express Ruby'**
H: 9–12 in (23–30 cm)
Large purple flowers with dark throats.

Phlox drummondii
H: 6–12 in (15–30 cm); S: 4 in (10 cm)
Annual, available in pink, mauve, and red. Plant out late May to June. Prefers moist sunny or partially shaded conditions.

Phyllitis scolopendrium
(syn. ***Asplenium scolopendrium***)
H: 12–18 in (30–45 cm); S: 18 in (45 cm); Z: 5–9.
Fern with light green elegantly curved fronds. Pot February to March. Water freely March to October. Overwinter in a greenhouse or conservatory. Prefers shade.

***Pittosporum tenuifolium* 'Purpureum'**
H: 6 ft (1.8 m); S: 13 ft (4 m); Z: 8–10
Evergreen large shrub or small tree. Pale green leaves change gradually to deep bronze purple. Honey-scented flowers in spring. Can be cut back.

Polygala myrtifolia
H and S: 5 ft (1.5 m)
Flowering evergreen shrub with pale green leaves and bright purple pea flowers. Overwinter in a greenhouse or conservatory.

Primula (Primrose)
A genus of annuals, perennials and biennials that generally enjoy sunny positions and well-drained soil. Characterized by basal leaves and primrose-shaped flowers.
P. vulgaris
H: 6 in (15 cm); S: 10 in (25 cm); Z: 5–8
Perennial with short thick leaves and pale yellow flowers with darker centers in late winter and spring. Looks good as a single plant or in shallow containers in clumps.
P. denticulata
H: 12–18 in (30–45 cm); Z: 4–8
Perennial that comes in shades of mauve or white with round heads on long stems in spring and has long toothed leaves. Works well as a single specimen plant.

P. veris (Cowslip)
H and S: 6–8 in (15–20 cm); Z: 5–8
Native perennial with rounded long leaves and small, deep yellow flowers in long-stalked clusters in spring.
***P. polyanthus* Gold Lace Group**
(Gold laced polyanthus)
H: 6–8 in (15–20 cm); Z: 3–8
Spring-flowering perennial with round heads in a variety of gold-edged colors. A large number of named varieties exist, hybridized since the mid-18th century.

Prunus lusitanica (Portugal laurel)
H and S: 20 ft (6 m); Z: 7–10
Evergreen shrub or small tree with ovate dark green glossy leaves and small white hawthorn-scented flowers in June. Small red fruits turning to dark purple in fall. A good subject for mop-head standards. Tolerates shade.

Pyracantha coccinea
H and S: 12 ft (4 m); Z: 6–9
Evergreen shrub, densely branched with white flowers in large clusters in summer followed by red or orange-red berries in large bunches in fall to winter. Prune to keep a compact shape; can be espaliered or pruned. Tolerant of all exposures, pollution and shade.

Rosa 'Sanders' White Rambler'

Rosa 'The Fairy'

Sempervivum tectorum

Rhododendron
H: 6–8 ft (2–2.5 m); Z: 5–8
Mainly evergreen shrubs with glossy foliage. Spring to summer flowering in a range of colors. Deadhead after flowering. Prune in April to keep in shape. Good hybrids for containers are: 'Cunningham's White' (white), 'Cynthia' (rose-crimson), 'Doncaster' (crimson-scarlet).

Rosa (Rose)
A genus of deciduous or semi-evergreen shrubs and scrambling climbers. Grown for flowers that are often fragrant. Plant in well-drained soil.

***R.* 'Sanders' White Rambler'**
H: 4–5 ft (1.2–1.5 m); Z: 4–9
Small scented white flowers in cascading clusters. Available as a container-grown weeping standard.

***R.* 'The Fairy'**
H: 2 ft (60 cm); S: 4 ft (120 cm); Z: 4–9
Polyantha spreading rose good for shallow containers. Clusters of beadlike buds that open to globular pink flowers through summer. Shade tolerant. Available as pot-grown standard and half-standard.

***R.* 'Nozomi'**
H: 2 ft (60 cm); Z: 5–9
Ground cover rose with small pearly-pink to white flowers produced in abundance. Ideal for hanging over the edge of pots.

***R.* 'White pet'**
H: 2 ft (60 cm); Z: 4–9
A 19th-century Polyantha short-growing rose producing huge trusses of pure white pompom-like blooms throughout summer. This rose will tolerate a shaded position. Available as a container-grown standard and half-standard.

Rudbeckia hirta (Cone flower)
H: 2–3 ft (60–90 cm); Z: 4–8
Golden-yellow flowers with dark brown center and long oblong leaves. Plant in a sunny position and water regularly.

***Salvia farinacea* 'Rhea'**
H: 3 ft (1 m); S: 1 ft (30 cm); Z: 9–10
A perennial with lance-shaped mid-green leaves and violet to blue flowers, from tubular spikes. Prefers well-drained soil and a sunny position.

Sempervivum tectorum (Houseleek)
H and S: 12 in (30 cm); Z: 3–8
Perennial succulent. Forms dense green mound of foliage suitable for a dry sunny position and will survive with virtually no soil and very little water. Good cascading display that works well in architectural designs in urns.

Senecio cineraria
(syn. ***Cineraria maritima***)
(Sea ragwort)
H and S: 1 ft (30 cm); Z: 8–10
Summer-flowering perennial. Has deeply cut gray leaves and yellow flowers midsummer to fall. 'Silver Dust' is a good non-flowering cultivar.

Tagetes erecta (African marigold)
H: 1–3 ft (30–100 cm)
Annual with single yellow or orange daisylike flowers. Long summer flowering. Plant out in May in a sunny position in well-drained soil, and water regularly.

Tilia* x *europea (Linden)
H: up to 100 ft (31 m); Z: 4–7
Deciduous tree with yellowish-white fragrant flowers and broadly ovate leaves. Easy to train in containers and can be pleached, pollarded, and generally kept in shape by hard pruning in mid- to late summer. If planting a bare-rooted linden, plant between mid-fall and spring.

***Tilia platyphyllos* 'Rubra'**
(Red-twigged linden)
H: up to 100 ft (31 m); Z: 4–7
Deciduous tree. Young shoots are bright brownish-red and make a particularly effective display in winter.

Trachelospermum jasminoides

Trachelospermum jasminoides
H and S: up to 21 ft (6.5 m); Z: 9–10
Slow-growing climbing shrub with narrowly oval dark, shiny green leaves and very fragrant white flowers over a long period from late spring to fall. Likes sun and moist soil. Overwinter indoors. Can be trained.

Verbena tenera
(Italian verbena)
H: 6–18 in (15–45 cm); S: 1 ft (30 cm); Z: 7–9
Summer flowering trailing perennial with blue or violet fragrant flowers. Also trailing V*erbena. tenuisecta* f. *alba* in white. Plant in well-drained soil in a sunny position.

Vinca minor
(Creeping myrtle)
H: 6 in (15 cm); S: 5 ft (1.5 m); Z: 7–9
Evergreen trailing shrub with blue to purple small white-centered flowers. V. *minor* 'Alba Variegata' produces white flowers. Likes semi-shade and moist soil.
***V. minor* 'Azurea Flore Plena'**
H: 6 in (15 cm); S: 5 ft (1.5 m); Z: 7–9
Evergreen trailing shrub. Bright sky-blue flowers on short flowering shoots in spring or summer. Leaves form a dense dark green mat. Best in sun and moist soil.

care and maintenance

EQUIPMENT

FOR THE GARDENER

Many of the projects in this book can be undertaken with the bare essentials of gardening equipment.

Use a wheelbarrow for fetching and moving pots and mixing soil, and a hand truck or dolly for transporting larger containers. A heavy-duty drop cloth or a specially made cloth with handles makes cleanup easier.

Indispensable hand tools include an old kitchen knife for weeding containers, a hand fork and trowel, a dibble to make holes for seeds or young plants, pruners, sharp scissors, shears, and a pruning saw.

Old garden tools are often much more satisfying to work with than new ones; you can buy them cheaply from secondhand stores. Failing that, invest in some stainless-steel tools, which wear well and are easy to clean.

For watering, you will need a watering can and a garden hose. Use a hose-end sprayer to apply liquid fertilizers and pesticides.

Gardening can be a grubby business and harsh on the hands, so wear gardening gloves for protection.

FOR THE WOODWORKER

There are not many complicated procedures in the construction projects described in this book. If you can put a piece of wood and screw separate pieces together, you will be able to manage most of them—but seek professional advice if you are in any doubt.

When buying and cutting wood, use English measurements. Metric sizes are also provided. Please note that in some cases the conversions are not direct. If your lumberyard uses English measurements, stick with inches and feet.

Use a hand saw (crosscut) or a circular saw for cutting lumber and plywood to size. A workbench or a sturdy pair of sawhorses are useful when cutting. A sabersaw is especially handy when making curved cuts, but a coping saw will also do the job.

The most versatile type of hammer is the claw hammer, which has one end for driving nails and a curved claw for removing them.

For drilling holes, use a power drill or a brace and bit. Most structures are secured with screws. A screwdriver with a Phillips head is recommended.

Also useful are a pair of C-clamps (for keeping work steady or holding pieces together) and a block plane.

FOR PAINTING

Ordinary household paintbrushes are all that is required for most of the projects, but for decorative details, an artist's brush will give more accuracy.

Before you begin to paint, make sure the surface is smooth and clean;

a soft-bristled dusting brush works best. Use mineral spirits to clean oil-based paint from brushes.

Other items of general equipment that may be useful include old rags and protective plastic or paper drop cloths. Exterior-grade wood filler can be used to fill cracks and indents.

FOR METAL PROJECTS

The metal constructions described in this book are relatively simple and need only a few special items of equipment, such as a pair of tin cutters for cutting lead or sheet metal facings and trimmings.

A hacksaw is the best tool for cutting thicker metals. When shaping metal, use a vise on a bench together with a mallet to help bend the strips and form corners.

For gilding, a range of metal leaf (in gold, silver, aluminum, and other metals) is available. When handling lead, wear a pair of protective gloves.

WOODWORKING

LUMBER

Lumber is broadly classified into two categories: softwood and hardwood. Softwood—which comes from a variety of coniferous trees—is suitable for many of the projects in this book because it is inexpensive and relatively easy to work with.

Before applying any other finish to the softwood, treat it with exterior-grade wood preservative.

Lumber is available with two types of surfaces: rough-sawn and surfaced (smooth). When buying lumber, be sure to specify what you want. Rough-sawn wood is good for certain treatments, especially if you plan to use a decorative stain or want a rustic look. Surfaced lumber is better for wood that will be painted, especially if you plan to use high-gloss paint.

Softwood comes in several different grades. For most projects, you will want "select," which is free of defects and knots. Exterior-grade plywood is available in several thicknesses: $^{3}/_{8}$, $^{1}/_{2}$, $^{5}/_{8}$, and $^{3}/_{4}$ in.

Oak and teak are the best hardwoods for outdoor use, but they are expensive and hard to work with. Use a stained finish with oak and teak; it is difficult to keep paint on these woods for the long term.

Lumber is sold by what's called "nominal size," which is the size of the wood (thickness x width) before it is milled. For instance, what is commonly referred to as a 2 x 4 is actually $1^{1}/_{2}$ x $3^{1}/_{2}$ in. (Length is not diminished by processing.) The projects in this book feature the nominal size in square brackets [] when applicable. Sizes indicated on lumber are actual dimensions—not nominal sizes.

GLUES AND FASTENERS

The adhesive recommended for use in the projects is waterproof carpenter's glue. Before gluing, always make sure the surfaces are free of dust and grease. Let the adhesive dry overnight to achieve its full strength.

Phillips screws are easiest to work with, especially when using an electric screwdriver. Choose screws that are plated to protect them from rust.

When you are screwing two pieces of wood together, start with a bit that is slightly smaller than the screw. Drill a pilot hole from the first piece and into the second. Next, using a bit that matches the thickness of the screw, drill through the first piece only. Then attach the two pieces with the screw. If you are drilling into sound wood and are more than 2 in (50 mm) from an edge, it is usually safe to skip the pilot hole.

If you need to use nails, choose galvanized ones to prevent rust. For a neat finish, use a nail set to punch your nail below the surface of the wood and fill the indentation with wood putty.

PRESERVATIVES

Unpreserved wood should be treated with exterior-grade wood preservative, which prevents rot, insect damage and disease. Exterior-grade wood preservatives are toxic to plants, so they must be applied well in advance of planting.

PAINTS

An extensive range of paint types is available for exterior use on wood, including exterior-grade latex and oil-based paint.

For concrete and masonry you can use most types of paint, but there are also special formulations for concrete and masonry.

For metal, use specially formulated high-gloss metal paint.

STAINS

Stains, which look better in muted colors, are most effective on rough-sawn lumber. Choose a nonchalking, or sealer, type of stain.

CONTAINERS

When deciding what sort of pot to have in your garden, consider where in the garden you need plant interest and what sort of container would look good in that spot. To be appreciated from a distance, the pot needs to be bold and simple in outline. The height of the planting must also be decided in relation to the rest of the garden; generally, the taller the planting, the larger the container needed.

A container with elaborate decorative detailing is best put in a foreground location where it can be seen clearly, and the same applies to planting—complex plans using delicate plants are best seen up close, where their detail can be fully appreciated.

The color of your material should be chosen to harmonize with the house and the rest of the garden as well as with the intended planting scheme. As a general rule, materials that weather and get a patina are more appealing; hand-thrown terra cotta quickly takes on an aged look. Lead, stone, and cast stone also age gracefully, and the process can be speeded up by applying vinegar in the case of lead, and yogurt, milk, or liquid manure in the case of stone and cast stone. One way to age a pot quickly is to place it under trees.

Cast iron and wood both need to be painted or stained to preserve them. Use a faded blue-gray green, referred to as "Versailles blue," a color often seen on the shutters of old houses in Italy and France.

CARING FOR CONTAINERS

Containers need to be scrupulously cleaned and scrubbed before planting; scrub them well on the inside with clean water, but try to preserve any weathering on the outside.

Some containers are best used with plastic liners, especially if you change plants with the seasons. Plastic liners are particularly useful for large Versailles cases and urns.

If you are going to leave your terra cotta outside all year around, check that it is frostproof. In winter, even hardy plants in pots will need protection from frost—wrap the pot with burlap, straw, or bubble wrap (as shown below). Where plants are in liners, pack straw between the plastic pot and container for protection. In early fall or spring check the condition of your containers and repaint them if necessary.

All containers need good drainage. Make sure there are enough holes to let out excess moisture and put in a thin layer of pot shards or gravel in the base of pots.

PLANTING MEDIUM

Different plants require different types of soil. For semi-permanent plantings, use potting soil that has been amended with compost or well-rotted manure. For seasonal plantings, use multi-purpose potting soil.

Some plants have particular requirements. For instance, special soils are available for bulbs, and very gritty free-draining soil-based composts are recommended for some alpine and rock plants.

Peat-based soil mixtures are appropriate for containers because they are light, but they also have a tendency to dry out, so are unsuitable for plants that are hard to water. Loam-based mixtures offer a more stable alternative but carry more weight. Also available are bark, coir, and wood-fiber composts that work well in containers.

POTTING PLANTS

Make sure the size of container you choose complements the size of the planting—it needs to be large enough to contain the root ball and sustain growth.

Some plants dislike being repotted repeatedly and do not mind being root-bound, whereas others need to be regularly potted on as they grow. Most seasonal plantings, if properly fed and watered, can tolerate being in a confined pot.

When planting a shrub or tree, start off with a large container that will support its growth for a number of years. Some Versailles cases are specifically designed for ease of re-potting in that the sides can be removed. Such a design might be suitable for large plants, such as orange and lemon trees, camellias, and greenhouse tropicals.

When planting a multiple seasonal display, it may be necessary to crowd the plants to create the desired effect. This would not be appropriate for permanent plantings but in this case, as long as the roots have space to grow down, the plants will survive.

For permanent plantings, be more careful with root-ball placement. Single specimens should be placed in the center of the pot and packed down. Make sure the finished soil surface is at least 1 in (25 mm) below the top edge of the container so that there is space for a water reservoir. In the case of standards, choose a specimen with an upright and secure stem (stake if necessary) because it is difficult to correct this later.

Climbing plants can have supports fixed in the soil or to the pot—there is a wide choice of stakes, metal shapes, and trellis obelisks that you can construct yourself or buy ready-made.

FEEDING AND WATERING

In summer, watering is the key to successful container gardening. Small pots, particularly those made of terra cotta, dry out very quickly, and during spells of hot weather they will need watering twice a day—in the early morning and in the evening, to avoid sunburn to wet leaves. Water larger pots only once a day. Always soak the plant thoroughly by filling the reservoir at the top up to the brim. If you are using a hose, use one with a fine spray so that the water pressure does not wash away any soil.

Reduce watering as the growing season comes to an end. In winter most plants need only to be kept from drying out, so check them every few days to make sure they are still moist. In some cases plants that are dormant in winter prefer the soil to be almost dry. You can conserve moisture by placing a layer of mulch over the soil.

There are various methods for feeding container-grown plants. Slow-release granules are good for long-term plantings—sprinkle them onto the surface of the soil and work them into the top layer of the soil. Other chemical fertilizers can be mixed into the compost when planting. Liquid fertilizers are diluted in water and used as part of the watering regime. Foliar feeds are sprayed on for instant effect, and organic material can be used as a top dressing. Use home-made compost, well-rotted manure, or blood and bonemeal, applied during the growing season.

When fertilizing, always apply at the recommended rates. Also keep in mind that some plants thrive best in relatively poor soil.

PEST AND DISEASES

Plants that are stressed by poor watering and feeding are more vulnerable to attack—so the surest way to prevent the invasion of pests and diseases is to take the best possible care of your plants and containers; cleanliness of pots and tools helps to keep bacterial diseases at bay, as does keeping a regular eye on their health.

Plants are vulnerable to three groups of diseases: bacterial, fungal, and viral, the last of which is untreatable—destruction of the plant is the only remedy.

The illustrations above show typical examples of bacterial leaf spot (left) and powdery mildew (right). Benomyl is the most useful spray for bacterial leaf spot, blackspot, fungal leaf spot, and powdery mildew; spray only on calm days after sunset so as not to harm beneficial insects.

The most common pests to attack container plants are aphids (greenfly and blackfly); these can be sprayed with insecticidal soap or neem-based sprays. Always identify the pest before using any treatment.

Store sprays and chemicals away from children and pets, and wear gloves and a mask as directed.

resources

USA

PLANT SUPPLIERS AND NURSERIES

Viette Nurseries
994 Long Meadow Road
Fisherville, VA 22939
(800) 575-5538
www.inthegardenradio.com

Avant Gardens
710 High Hill Road
North Dartmouth
MA 02747-1363
(508) 998-8819
www.avantgardensne.com

Bluestone Perennials
7211 Middle Ridge Road
Madison, OH 44057-3096
(800) 852-5243
www.bluestoneperennials.com

Carroll Gardens
444 E. Main St.
Westminster, MD 21157
(410) 876-7336
www.carrollgardens.com

Completely Clematis
217 Argilla Road
Ipswich, MA 01938-2617
(978) 356-3197
www.clematisnursery.com

Dutch Gardens
P.O. Box 2999
Bloomington, IL 61702-2999
(800) 944-2250
www.dutchgardens.com

Eastern Plant Specialties
320 Bay Point Rd
Georgetown, ME 04548
(207) 607-1284
www.easternplant.blog

Glasshouse Works
Church St., P.O. Box 97
Stewart, OH 45778-0097
(740) 662-2142
www.rareplants.com

Goodwin Creek Gardens
970 Cedar Flat Rd
Williams, OR 97544
(800) 846-7357
www.goodwincreekgardens.com

The Great Outdoors
2730 S. Congress Avenue
Austin, TX 78704-6422
(512) 448-2992
www.gonursery.com

Heronswood Nursery
7530 NE 288th St.
Kingston, WA 98346
(360) 297-9620
www.heronswood.com

Lilypons Water Gardens
6800 Lilypons Road
Adamstown, MD 21710
(800) 999-5459
www.lilypons.com

Logee's Greenhouses
141 North St.
Danielson, CT 06239
(888) 330-8038
www.logees.com

McClure & Zimmerman
108 W. Winnebago
P.O. Box 368
Friesland, WI 53935-0368
(800) 883-6998
www.mzbulb.com

Miller Nurseries
5060 West Lake Road
Canandaigua, NY 14424
(800) 836-9630
www.starkbros.com

Plant Delights Nursery
9241 Sauls Rd.
Raleigh, NC 27603
(919) 772-4794
www.plantdelights.com

Wayside Gardens
Garden Lane
Hodges, SC 29695-0001
(800) 845-1124
www.waysidegardens.com

White Flower Farm
P.O. Box 50
Litchfield, CT 06759
(800) 503-9624
www.whiteflowerfarm.com

MATERIALS AND TOOLS

Ace Hardware Corporation
2200 Kensington Ct.
Oak Brook, IL 60523-2100
(866) 290-5334
www.acehardware.com
Hardware from A to Z with seasonal gardening supplies.

Lowe's Home Centers
Located throughout the U.S.A.
(800) 445-6937
www.lowes.com
A nationwide chain warehouse of home improvement supplies.

The Home Depot
2455 Paces Ferry Road SE
Atlanta, GA 30339
(770) 433-8211
www.homedepot.com
Chain store with home and garden supplies and materials.

Sears, Roebuck
(800) MY-SEARS
www.sears.com
Garden products available through catalog, retail outlets, and online store.

GARDEN SUPPLIES

Dan's Garden Shop
5821 Woodwinds Circle
Frederick, MD 21703
(301) 695-5966

Gardener's Supply Company
128 Intervale Rd.
Burlington, VT 05401
(888) 833-1412
www.gardeners.com
Tools, containers, soil, seed, and everything for the garden.

Kinsman Company
River Road
Point Pleasant
PA 18950-0357
(800) 733-4146
www.kinsmangarden.com
Classy garden items, including moss-lined baskets.

Kmart
(800) 355-6388
www.kmart.com
Chain store with locations throughout the U.S.A. Gardening supplies and seasonal flowers.

LaBrake's Garden Path and Pond
8 Pitt St.
Brushton, NY 12916
(518) 529-8972
www.gardenponds.com

Walt Nicke's Garden Talk
P.O. Box 433
Topsfield, MA 01983
(978) 887-3388
www.gardentalk.com
Fine tools and garden ornaments.

CONTAINERS

Brooks Barrel Company
5228 Bucktown Rd.
P.O. Box 1056
Cambridge, MD 21613
(410) 228-0790
Handcrafted wooden barrels, kegs and planters of all sizes.

Karen Harris
200 East Genesee St.
Fayetteville, NY 13066
(315) 635-8209
Handmade hypertufa garden troughs.

Master Garden Products
15650 SE 9th St.
Bellevue, WA 98008
(425) 401-1083
www.mastergardenproducts.com

Windowbox.com
6056 Corte Del Cedro
Carlsbad, CA 92011
(888) GARDEN-Box
www.windowbox.com
Especially for the rooftop or balcony gardener; online advice.

CRAFTS

Ben Franklin
Nationwide franchises
(808) 838-7773
www.hmstores.com
Craft supplies galore, including different sized pine cones.

Michael's
850 North Lake Dr., Suite
500 Coppell, TX 75019
(972) 304-6200
www.michaels.com
An arts and crafts store; good source for metal leaf.

Target Stores
33 South Sixth Street
Minneapolis, MN 55402
(612) 304-8000
www.target.com
Modern variety store with craft needs and slightly sophisiticated plastic.

UK

PAINTS AND STAINS

Farrow and Ball
Uddens Estate, Wimborne
Dorset BH21 7NI
01202 876141
www.farrow-ball.com

John Oliver Ltd
33 Pembridge Road
London W11 3HG
020 7221 6466

Sikkens UK Ltd
Meadow Lane, St Ives
Cambridgeshire PE27 4UY
01480 496868

NURSERIES

Blooms of Bressingham
Dorney Court
Dorney, Windsor
Berkshire SL4 6QP
01628 669999
And at nine other locations in southern and central England.

Capital Gardens
Alexandra Palace Garden
Centre Alexandra Palace
Way
London N22 7BB
020 8444 2555
www.capitalgardens.co.uk

The Chelsea Gardener
125 Sydney Street
London SW3 6NR
020 7352 5656

Deacons Nursery
Moor View, Godshill
Isle of Wight PO38 3HW
01983 840750

Finchley Nurseries
Burton Hole Lane
London NW7 1AS
020 8959 2124

Garson Farm Garden Centre
Winterdown Road, Esher
Surrey KT10 8LS
01372 460181

Highfield Nurseries
Whitminster
Gloucester
Gloucestershire GL2 7PB
01452 741444

Longacres Nursery
London Road, Bagshot
Surrey GU19 5JB
01276 476778

Potterton & Martin
Moortown Road, Nettleton
Market Rasen
Lincolnshire LN7 6HX
01472 851714

The Romantic Garden
Nursery
Swannington
Norwich
Norfolk NR9 5NW
01603 261488
www.romantic-garden-nursery.co.uk

Scotts Nurseries
Merriott
Somerset TA16 5PL
01460 72306

Syon Park Garden Centre
Syon Park
Brentford
Middlesex TW8 8JG
020 8568 7776

The Van Hage Garden Co.
Bragbury End
Stevenage
Hertfordshire SG2 8TJ
01438 811777

Wyevale Garden Centres
Waddon Way
Purley Way
Croydon CR0 4HY
020 8688 5117

TERRACOTTA AND STONEWARE

Chilstone
Victoria Park
Fordcombe
Kent TN3 0RD
01892 740866

Christie's
8 King Street
London SW1Y 6QT
020 7839 9060

Cranborne Stone
Butts Pond
Sturminster Newton
Dorset DT10 1AZ
01258 472685

Pots and Pithoi
The Barns, East Street
Turners Hill
West Sussex RH10 4QA
01342 714793

Whichford Pottery
Whichford
Shipston-on-Stour
Warwickshire CV36 5PG
01608 684416

PLANTERS AND GARDEN STRUCTURES

Baileys Home & Garden
The Engine Shed
Ashburton Industrial Estate
Ross-on-Wye
Herefordshire HR9 7BW
01989 561939

Bulbeck Foundry
Reach Road, Burwell
Cambridgeshire CB25 0GH
01638 743153

Exmoor Baskets & Hurdles
The Farmhouse
Poole Farm, Exebridge
Dulverton
Somerset TA22 9BQ
01398 323391

George Carter
Silverstone Farm
North Elmham
Norfolk NR20 5EX
01362 668130

Interior Landscaping
Products
The Sussex Barn
New Lodge Farm
Hooe, Battle
East Sussex TN33 9HJ
01424 844444
www.interiorlandscaping.co.uk

Rayment Wirework
Hoo Farm, Monkton Road
Ramsgate
Kent CT12 4JB
01843 821628

Stuart Garden Architecture
Burrow Hill Farm
Wiveliscombe
Somerset TA4 2RN
01984 667458

Terrace and Garden
Maces Farm
Rickling Green
Saffron Walden
Essex CB11 3YG
01799 543289

TIMBER AND BUILDING SUPPLIES

B & Q
Chestnut Ave
Chandlers Ford
Eastleigh
Hampshire SO53 3LE
0333 014 3098
www.diy.com
Over 320 stores nationwide.

Homebase
0345 077 8888
www.homebase.co.uk
Over 300 stores nationwide.

E. K. Wilson & Sons
86 Old Brompton Road
Kensington, London SW7 3LQ
020 7589 0046

The York Handmade Brick
Company
Winchester House
Forest Lane, Alne
North Yorkshire YO61 1TU
01347 838881
www.yorkhandmade.co.uk

index

credits

The projects in this book were designed by George Carter, except for Vertical Planting (pages 24–27) and A Wirework Hanging Basket (pages 58–61), both of which were designed by Jane Seabrook at The Chelsea Gardener, London, UK. Much of the planting was lent by John Powles at the Romantic Garden Nursery, Swannington, Norfolk, UK. All the photographs were taken by Marianne Majerus, except for page 45 bottom right, which was taken by Francesca Yorke at an Islington garden designed by Diana Yakeley, Yakeley Associates Design, Interior and Garden Design, 13 College Cross, London N1 1YY, UK (+ 44(0)20 7609 9846) dy@yakeley.com.

acknowledgments

The author would like to thank the many people involved in making this book, particularly Marianne Majerus for her wonderful photographs, John Powles and The Romantic Garden Nursery for the loan of plants, and Jane Seabrook and The Chelsea Gardener for planting and use of the nursery.

The following people kindly lent their own beautiful gardens as backdrops for photography: Mrs David Cargill, Ethne Clarke, Mr and Mrs Robert Clarke, Viscount and Viscountess De L'Isle, Major Charles Fenwick, Mrs Clive Hardcastle, Mr and Mrs Derek Howard, Anne Ryland, Jacqui Small, The Lady Tollemache, and Mr and Mrs Richard Winch.

Thanks also go to Jill Duchess of Hamilton for lending urns, to Jill Hamer for typing the text, and to Peter Goodwins and Jack Bell for construction and bricklaying.

The first edition of this book was edited by Toria Leitch and designed by Ingunn Jensen.